Puffin Books

King Death's Garden

Maurice was furious with ......
Middle East and leaving ...... (for the time being) behind. He didn't want to go to the Gulf – why couldn't his
father just stay in England and be unemployed, he
thought. But he wasn't too happy about being dumped
on ancient, spidery Great Aunt Ada instead. The only
thing that might make the rest of the school year bear-
able would be a friendship with the girl he admired from
afar: the elegant Jasmin Kapoor, with her glossy swept-
back hair and stylish leggings. But she was a year older
than Maurice, and kept herself so aloof that the chance
of getting to know her seemed pretty remote.

After a bit, Maurice found he quite liked living with
Aunt Ada. He liked the calm, permanent feeling of the
old house. He enjoyed walking to and from school
through the cemetery at the foot of the garden, and, in
his spare time, exploring all its alleys and byways. He
was intrigued by the strange, ragged girl he met in the
cemetery. He was also keen to learn more about the old
scientist who claimed to have made a great discovery,
but who burnt all his papers before he died without
revealing what the discovery was. If Aunt Ada knew
anything, she wasn't telling – but Maurice, by now, had
stumbled on the discovery himself. He was gradually
getting to spend more and more time in the hidden green
hollow where amazing experiences came to him, forgetting about Jasmin, forgetting his tormenting asthma
and all his other problems. Maybe the cemetery didn't
always seem so harmless now, but Maurice wasn't going
to listen to anyone who warned him against too strong
an obsession with King Death's Garden.

This absorbing story, stepping skilfully between the
robust everyday world of school and play and the eerie
other world that comes to dominate Maurice, will de-
light imaginative readers.

Ann Halam is the pen name of Gwyneth Jones, who
writes science fiction for adults. She was brought up in
the North of England, is married and lives in Brighton.

ANN HALAM

KING DEATH'S GARDEN

A GHOST STORY

PUFFIN BOOKS

PUFFIN BOOKS

Penguin Books Ltd, 27 Wrights Lane, London w8 5TZ (Publishing and Editorial)
and Harmondsworth, Middlesex, England (Distribution and Warehouse)
Viking Penguin Inc., 40 West 23rd Street, New York, New York 10010, USA
Penguin Books Australia Ltd, Ringwood, Victoria, Australia
Penguin Books Canada Ltd, 2801 John Street, Markham, Ontario, Canada L3R 1B4
Penguin Books (NZ) Ltd, 182–190 Wairau Road, Auckland 10, New Zealand

First published by Orchard Books 1986
Published in Puffin Books 1988

Copyright © Ann Halam, 1986
All rights reserved

The publishers would like to thank The Literary Trustees of Walter de la Mare and
The Society of Authors as their representative for permission to reprint the extract
from *Henry Brocken* by Walter de la Mare

Printed and bound in Great Britain by
Cox & Wyman Ltd, Reading

I met once an earnest and yet very popular young gentleman by the name of Science, who explained almost everything on earth to me so clearly, so patiently, and fatherly I thought I should evermore sleep in peace. But we met at noon.

Henry Brocken, Walter De La Mare

One

Unfortunately neither of Maurice's parents could be with him the day he moved house. His father had already gone to the Gulf and his mother had left two days ago with the baby. It could not be helped. Aunt Sue and Uncle Tom collected him and carried him away, leaving him with a brief impression of Mum neatly stowing herself and all the baby stuff into a taxi. She gave Maurice a kiss and a hug, and at the last moment he relented and hugged her back, just in case the plane crashed. The last thing he heard her say was "This is going to cost a fortune". She was talking to the taxi driver, but she sounded choked. Maurice was glad. She deserved to be upset.

It was not going to cost a fortune to board Maurice because he was going to live with his great aunt. Aunt Sue and Uncle Tom had arranged to take him home with them for a couple of nights, but there wasn't enough room for him to stay. After two nights on the campbed between cousins Mark and Ben, he'd had quite enough of that arrangement. There were no other relatives within reach.

In the turmoil of the great change, no one had considered that Maurice had not actually seen his great aunt for years. She lived up a hill, away from the shopping streets of Brighton; and quite remote from the estate on the edge of the downs which was Maurice's home ground. As Uncle Tom drove along, passing street corners nudged at Maurice's memory. He recalled the taste of a chocolate cream bar he had never liked. That was what his great aunt used to give him. The car drew up in a quiet little street, above red tiled pastel-walled crescents and the blue line of the sea. They all went in and Maurice sat looking round his great aunt's parlour while his aunt and uncle talked.

He could tell they were a bit worried. Maurice's fate had been decided weeks ago, although he himself had never believed it would actually happen. But now that the moment had come Great Aunt looked very aged and wavery. She ought to be in a home, thought Maurice. They can't leave me here.

"I have my home help," said Great Aunt.

She was exactly the way he remembered her, thin and spidery and peering. She must be so old she had stopped changing.

"Oh yes, the home help," remembered his aunt with relief.

"For the rough cleaning. That's what they call themselves nowadays. The Council arranges it."

Maurice let the conversation float away over his head, a trick he had perfected years ago, and looked at great aunt's wallpaper which was covered in huge floppy pink roses. It was a very old-fashioned parlour, with a piano and a round table covered with a velvet cloth: a tiny old writing desk and four swollen and uncomfortable armchairs, one of which Maurice was sitting on. The thick curtains at the front windows were opened very grudgingly, letting in two narrow bars of thin sunshine. The piano had candle-holders on either side of the music rest, the round table had a large groping sort of fern sitting in the middle of it. Maurice began to count roses.

"Of course, he was quite famous in his field," said the old lady, picking up a framed photograph from beside the fern. "But unfortunately he was rather eccentric. He burned his papers, you know."

She was telling his aunt and uncle the story behind this house. It had belonged many years ago to a retired scientist. He had almost been famous. He retired to the seaside for his health and Maurice's great aunt was his housekeeper. He was supposed to be researching a great invention, but no one knew what, because he went slightly mad and destroyed all his work just a few years before he died. He left Great Aunt the house.

"It's a very interesting story," said Uncle Tom, holding the picture respectfully. "What was his field again? I'm afraid I've forgotten."

"Alas, I couldn't say, my dear," answered Great Aunt. "I was merely his housekeeper." She took the picture back firmly and replaced it exactly in the mark it had made on the faded velvet.

Uncle Tom must have heard the old legend hundreds of times. He was just being polite. But Great Aunt Ada, Maurice remembered vaguely, was supposed to be touchy about it. There was some family gossip, he thought – the kind considered unsuitable for children. He glanced at the old lady speculatively: but it was hard to picture her in a steamy love affair. His mind wandered, he remembered he would be able to walk to school from here. That was a tiny plus, because he hated the squalid uproar on school buses.

"It will be a big change for you, having a young boy living here," suggested Aunt Sue nervously.

"Oh, I don't mind," said Great Aunt. "Maurice is a quiet child, I'm sure I'll enjoy his stay. There are things he can do for me."

She looked at Maurice and smiled. Her glasses were crooked, and mended on one side with a bit of pink sticking plaster. How does she know I'm a quiet child? thought Maurice. She hasn't seen me since I was eight. However, he smiled back. He counted the old lady less to blame than the rest of them. Then he was sent upstairs to unpack while the grown ups had a grown up conversation – though it seemed to Maurice his aunt and uncle had already run out of steam.

There was a good reason why Maurice couldn't go with his family to the Gulf, at least not right away. He suffered from asthma, and a plague of allergies: not desperately, but enough to keep him out of school quite often. It interrupted his work, so everyone thought it was wrong to take him away, on top of all that, in the middle of the school year. There was an International School in the neighbouring state, where he could be a weekly boarder. It was hoped he would start there in the autumn term.

"What's a weekly boarder?" Maurice had asked.

"You come home every weekend."

"Home? To England?"

"Oh, Maurice, let's not go through all that again."

Maurice did not want to go to the Middle East at all. He had been fighting a desperate rearguard action since the idea first crawled into the light, out of the uncertain realm of suspicious envelopes and muted conversations that stopped when he appeared. He hated, hated, hated this job that Dad had found. He would rather starve. Why couldn't they all go on the dole? Other people did. Up until the very last days he had been sure he had won a partial victory. He might have lost Dad except for the holidays, but he'd kept Mum at home. He couldn't believe she would leave him. But she did. He detested baby Tabitha, for being so portable. His affection for her had always been a little shaky, and based mainly on the hope that she would slow Mum down a bit (she had not, noticeably).

He put his diet sheet beside his inhaler with his latest antihistamines and the rest of his survival kit. "The truth is," the doctor said, "most of it you'll grow out of and some of it you'll get used to. Meanwhile, we try and distract you with our so-called cures." The treacherous pig also claimed the dry air of the Gulf would do wonders for his wheezing.

He pinned a map of the Middle East on the wall and sat on the end of the bed contemplating it. The Do'an was the name of the state. It was part of the Arab Emirates. His father was based in a town called Ishar, on the coast. Hot, and full of skyscrapers. Sadly, said Dad, they had pulled most of the old town to bits, to make room for progress. Mum and little Tabby-brat were also there by now. He put in a red pin to mark Ishar, and thought viciously of wax dolls. He put his photographs on the chest of drawers under the map. There was his mother, in white shorts and a raggy teeshirt, on the boat in Norfolk last summer: full of health and energy. Maurice had spent that holiday battened down under the hatches, or staggering around with an antihistamine head full of cotton wool. The baby was tucked into a corner of Mum's picture. She wasn't a bad baby, she showed signs of intelligence. He had been hoping to develop her to read books and so on eventually, before Mum's influence could turn her into a sporting idiot. No good thinking of that now.

The indignity of it! Not even a grandmother. A great aunt.

After a few minutes he took the red pin out, a little guiltily. It looked too much as if it was marking a battlefield. He put a green one in instead, that seemed more hopeful. Map and pins had been provided by Mum, among other peace offerings. But a moment later he flung himself down on the bed, scowling. He would never forgive them, never. They had ruined his life.

The discussion downstairs went on a for a while. He lay on his new bed half dozing: he didn't want to go down and hear himself being talked about. The house was very quiet. A clock was ticking somewhere, steadily and gently. There's something about this place, he decided. It's peaceful. He pictured the floppy pink roses and the velvet tablecloth and wondered if everything was exactly as it had been when the old scientist lived here. Perhaps Great Aunt had kept it the same, in memory. It was rather a spooky thought but he didn't seem to mind . . . At last his relations could be heard coming out into the hall, being called Susan and Thomas in Great Aunt's thin precise voice, which sounded odd. Their feet thumped up the stairs and they stood in the open door.

In the bitterness of his feelings Maurice hardly bothered to look at them.

"Oh, you're having a rest," said Aunt Sue. "Sorry –"

"We're going now."

"If you need anything you just phone us straight away. We'll come and see you on Monday about six, to make sure you've settled in."

"He'll be all right. Maurice is OK."

Then they were gone. He heard them talking quietly, in off duty voices, as they went down the stairs.

"I hope it's not too much for her."

"There's the home help. And we'll keep an eye on things."

"Funny sort of place to live, isn't it?"

"Oh, I don't know. Plenty of free fresh flowers."

Laughter. Bang of the front door. Vrrm of the car starting up and driving away.

When the quiet and the ticking clock had returned, Maurice sat up. He could hear his great aunt moving about gently, probably in the kitchen. After all, I could be at boarding school, he thought. Or in a children's home, seeing as I've been abandoned. He wondered what his aunt meant about the flowers. It was an odd thing to say. He got off his bed and went to the window, which overlooked the back of the house. The dark curtains were open, but there was a crusty veil of yellowed lace. He pushed it aside and stood looking down at the garden and beyond the garden, over a wall, into what looked at first like a park. But then he saw the grey shadows on the green grass in their regular solemn rows and he smiled wryly, seeing the joke. Of course. It was the cemetery.

Maurice went to school on Monday as if nothing had happened. But he remembered all through the day that he wasn't going home and it gave him an odd empty feeling in his stomach. He had spoken to his mother and father on Sunday night: they had rung up as arranged across the thousands of miles, from a different time. This is going to cost a fortune, he thought, and asked after the baby. She was all right.

Now there was no more suburban house with the floor

length front window and the cherry trees in its young garden. No more familiar street full of noisy little kids with trainer wheels on their bicycles. No more Maurice's room. It was let, it was going to be lived in by someone else. He had a mad thought he would run away home after school, and camp out in the untamed bit of the back garden until Mum and Dad came back – the wild boy of Keymer Drive. But he knew he wouldn't do it. He would get used to the quiet and the ticking clock and the lace curtains.

Maurice's school, Fairsea Comprehensive, stood opposite Brighton Racecourse, looking out over roofs and tower blocks to the windy channel. The green downs stood in folds above the seaside town, joined together at the top and deeply pleated in between. In the pleat between Fairsea and Great Aunt Ada's house was the big cemetery Maurice had seen from his bedroom window. Fairsea was called a Community Education Centre, which meant there was a swimming pool on the site, and a public library and squash courts. But the library only opened three days a week now, and the pool had had to be closed along with the squash courts.

The school had constant floods of splendid fresh air pouring over it, smelling of sea water when the wind was right. In the middle of the site was an old house that had been a convalescent home for children, long ago. It held club rooms and stockrooms now, and was surrounded by new flatroofed buildings and prefabs – no longer very new and leaking in the winter. The only interesting survival was a sort of out-of-doors classroom in a courtyard, with benches and desks in it so that the convalescent children could do their lessons in the healthy open air. It had not been used – officially – since (so the legend went) all the sick children died of pneumonia, but it made a mild adventure playground for the junior school.

It was Monday afternoon, time to go home. The library was open: on the forecourt outside Mrs Bollom, mother of a boy in Maurice's class, was talking to Mrs Wray, the librarian. Mrs Bollom smiled at Maurice, not knowing that the friendship between him and her son was long over. Maurice didn't make friends easily. His asthma and his allergies made him wary. But this boy used to be all right, until one day he broke an arrangement with Maurice, explaining he wanted to play football with some other friends who were "ordinary, like me".

That was it. Maurice was no longer on speaking terms with the ordinary boy.

Swinging on Mrs Bollom's arm, threatening to dislodge her library books, was the ordinary boy's little sister. She was five and very big for her age. She suffered from hyperactiveness: in simple terms she made everybody tired. Her name was Elizabeth, but even her own mother referred to her as Ghengis Khan. She didn't talk much, but whenever you had been with her you felt as if someone had been banging saucepan lids over your ears.

Mrs Wray and Mrs Bollom discussed Ghengis's diet as if she was a space shuttle and they were trying to get the rocket fuel right. Ghengis spotted Maurice and jumped on him. She didn't know that she wasn't supposed to know him any more. The boy moved off shiftily, but Maurice let Ghengis grab him. On a bench at the end of the forecourt his idol was sitting primly waiting for her parents. Being friendless, Maurice had to take any chance he could of hanging around.

Her name was Jasmin. She was in third year, a year above him and completely out of reach. She wore her hair brushed straight back into a great thick plait and springing up smooth and glossy above her forehead. She always wore carefully pressed immaculate school uniform, whereas nearly every other girl in the school fought steadily to infiltrate with hobble skirts, fishnet tights and general seediness. Jasmin wore close fitting leggings under her skirt, as she was entitled to do for her religion. Maurice thought nothing had ever looked so stylish. She had never spoken to him willingly. Both her parents were doctors. One or other of them dropped her off and collected her every day in a big dark car. She mixed solely with the other Asian girls, of whom there were a few in the school.

There was only one Asian boy of any note, in the fourth form. His father was a supermarket owner. He was called Aziz, and he had a face "like a movie star" – said Maurice's mother. She was given to making idiotic comments like that, at the school gates and far too loud. Jasmin showed no interest in Aziz, although he was said to admire her. But Maurice felt he had more to offer. True friendship, instead of the coarse thoughts bound to be on the mind of a fourth year with a face like a movie star. He lived in fear of a group of girls in his own year: a gang so terrible they were feared by half the school, including teachers, even though they were only juniors. If they ever found out what Maurice the weed was dreaming of, life would be unendurable.

He had told no one, he had more sense, that it was for Jasmin's sake that he couldn't bear to leave school and go to the Gulf. It wasn't exactly true anyway. But she was certainly one of the chief reasons. Now he had only four months left. Surely he could get up the courage to speak to her, at least once.

The monster child was delighted by Maurice's attention. He felt a pang of guilt, but didn't let it keep him from his plan. In another moment Jasmin was startled to find herself grabbed by the arm. Ghengis beamed at her. She had a grip like a vice: it could be quite frightening if you weren't used to it.

"What does your Mummy do?"

Jasmin stared. "She's a doctor," she answered faintly.

"What does your *Daddy* do?"

"He's a doctor," murmured Jasmin.

Ghengis scowled, tightening her hold like a tourniquet.

"I expect they must have had a lesson in her class," said Maurice, coming to the rescue. "How people earn their livings, you know. Postman Pat and all that –"

Jasmin smiled distantly.

"Is she your little sister?"

"No, just a friend." He corrected himself quickly, not wanting to sound eccentric. "A friend's little sister, I mean."

"Oh."

"Her Mummy's a doctor," said Ghengis. "Why did you want to know? Maurice – why did you want to know?"

Quickly Maurice swung her round by the arms, drowning this revealing inquiry in joyful squeals.

"My mother used to sell boats," he cried, as if it was part of the game. "Now she's going to teach scuba diving."

But Jasmin showed no interest at all in Maurice's fascinating mother. The dark car had appeared. A back door opened and she got in, without another glance. Maurice was left among the flotsam and jetsam of the end of school, with a monster five-year-old hauling his arms, feeling distinctly foolish. Failed again. Ghengis's brother was hiding behind his mother.

Mrs Wray, the librarian, beamed at Maurice.

"Well, Maurice, have you settled in at your great aunt's? D'you think you can find your way home?"

It was none of her business. She wasn't even a teacher.

"I don't think I'll get lost. It's just straight through the cemetery."

"Brr. Rather you than me. You'd better hurry off. You wouldn't want to be in there when it's getting dark."

"Why not?" said Maurice. "Actually, I like graveyards."

In the morning he'd hardly noticed it. He'd just walked in by one lot of gates and out the other, and been vaguely aware of trees and grass in between. He had been thinking of other things: that miserable phone call, and his plan to run away and live rough. But now, as he passed inside the big wrought iron gates and looked around, he found he had told the truth. He liked this place. The main path was a wide drive of red gravel, descending into the valley between Fairsea and great aunt's street. It led to the funeral church in the middle: a private road for long black flower-laden cars. On either side of the drive stood tall old beautiful trees, some of them still quite bare and some beginning to show budding leaves. He walked along slowly. It was very quiet. There were birds singing and their wings flirted occasionally over his head. In spite of what Mrs Wray had said it was nowhere near dark so he slowed down even more and looked at the gravestones.

This was the five star part of the cemetery, where the top people stayed. You could tell that by the handsome trees and smooth lawns. A lord mayor, a superintendent of police. A general, lots of vicars and ministers, lots of rich and charitable ladies. There were some fine memorials. One person had a life sized statue of a horse – or else it was the horse who was buried. There were weeping angels, child angels, angels holding lilies, angels clinging to anchors, angels with so much stone wing-span it was a wonder they could stand up. There were symbolic broken pillars and obelisks of shiny red granite. There was a family who had decided to live under an expanse of marble as big as a small skating rink, roped off with rusty iron chains. He imagined the angels climbing down from their stones to rollerskate, when there was no one around.

By the funeral church he turned up a flight of steps, dark and almost buried in shrubbery. He half hoped they might be secret: he had come across them this morning when he was looking for a short cut to the Fairsea side. There were two flights. He stopped in between on a dark moist patch under a holly tree. He had heard something rustling and wanted to see if there was a bird on a nest. The evergreen stirred again as he turned away and with the corner of his eye he caught a flash of bright colour: bigger than a robin or a bluetit. Perhaps a rare migrant. He waited, but it must have flown away.

At the top of the steps a flint wall divided five star from a lower class of accommodation. In the distance graves lay out in bare rows towards the horizon; but the way home for Maurice was through an older part where the grass was rough and tangled with brambles: and dotted with a few small homely trees. The gravestones sloped or propped each other comfort-ably. Some of the graves had settled in the middle, others had cheerful helpings of violent blue or acid green chippings. There were plastic flowers turning grey, in fat little urns called

17

MUM or OUR AUNTIE . . . Maurice decided he liked this side of the wall. But on the other hand the dark solemn part with the big trees was very impressive.

The Best Mum and Dad in the world . . . Never a Cross Word
. . . And in the morn the angel faces smile, That I have loved long
since and lost awhile . . . Love's last gift, Remembrance . . .

Suddenly he realised that someone was watching him. It made him jump, because just then he was well off the path and actually standing on a grave. He was only putting back some plastic flowers that had pathetically fallen out of their urn, but he knew it wouldn't look good. A big elderly man was standing by a bench just a few yards away. He was glaring like somebody in authority – maybe a gardener. Maurice retreated carelessly, pretending not to have noticed the stern stare. He wasn't doing anything wrong after all. He stepped round a couple of headstones – but then, when he looked up, the man was gone.

There was no one on the path, there was no one in sight. I imagined it, he thought. Unless he's gone off to fetch the vicar, or report me to the office or something. Maurice wandered on, admiring the primroses and crocuses that grew half wild in the rough brown winter grass. That old man must have sprinted to get out of sight so quickly . . . Perhaps I'm imagining things, he thought. My mind's giving way under the strain.

A faithful heart, a love so true . . . Reunited . . . Gone from our
lives but not from our hearts . . . The Great Physician came and
prescribed rest . . .

He stopped a while under a tree that had no buds, no leaves; only black blobs on its twigs. Its branches dangled almost to the ground like listless dry tentacles. The effect was probably supposed to be ornamental, but at the moment it looked as if it was dying. I know how you feel, said Maurice (not out loud). We don't fit, do we. There's no place for us in this world.

When he arrived "home" at the house with the lace curtains

he opened the door with his new latchkey and heard the piano tinkling. His great aunt was singing all by herself in a thin old lady's voice.

Oh mother, mother, make my bed
And make it cold and narrow . . .

Upstairs the old clock was ticking gently, gently.

Great Aunt Ada Drew had lived alone for a long time. The family rarely came to see her. But if she resented having a young relative suddenly dumped on her, after years of neglect, she was too polite to show it. Maurice decided to call her Aunt Ada: "Great Aunt" was too much of a mouthful. In practice, he called her nothing. He hardly spoke to her: she didn't seem to want much social contact.

Maurice had not expected Aunt Ada to know what to do with a boy. He had imagined – because he didn't take any notice when arrangements were being made, that he'd be fending for himself. But it didn't work out like that. There was a freezer in the outhouse that led off the kitchen, well stocked with things Maurice could eat. Someone had obviously been studying his diet sheet. It seemed Aunt Ada lived almost entirely on frozen food "because it was so much easier" but sometimes Maurice would find a colander of fresh vegetables waiting for him, with a note giving instructions such as "boil 5 mins" – in an unknown strong and curling handwriting. There was a washing machine too, and his dirty clothes began to disappear mysteriously.

Maurice wasn't curious. It seemed quite reasonable that there should be an invisible person living in this shadowy house. But halfway through the first week he came in from school on a dark rainy afternoon and heard a conversation going on: his great aunt and another voice, deep and strange, murmuring in the parlour where nothing had changed for forty years. For a moment it put shivers down the back of his neck, then he shrugged and walked past. If Aunt Ada wanted to make up a voice for her professor, to bring back memories, what harm was there in that? But the voices stopped, and the old fashioned portière curtain that hung inside the parlour door to keep out draughts was pulled back by a hand that could not be seen. Maurice almost yelled, but swallowed it in time. A heavily built black woman in a blue nylon overall leaned from her chair and smiled at him casually, then she dropped the curtain and went on talking to his aunt.

Of course, it was the home help. Her name was Mary. Maurice wasn't so lucky the next day. He came home earlier and was caught in his bedroom.

"So you're the niece's child," said Mary cheerfully, frankly looking him up and down as she tossed his bedclothes (which he had already tidied) into hospital order. "You really need all of this?"

Maurice felt flattened by her big capable hand, sweeping over his survival kit.

"It's asthma," he said. "They tried giving me injections, but it wasn't suitable."

"Huh."

She peered at the map of the Middle East.

"This where your family is? Why they leave you behind?"

"I've got to go to school –" began Maurice.

"Funny thing. I thought that warm dry air was good for the asthma."

He looked at her with dislike. "You don't have to do things for me. You're only supposed to help my great aunt, aren't you?"

"Oh, I do what I like." She laughed, and swept up a handful of dirty washing. "You better be careful in this house, young boy. You going to fade away just like your auntie."

"If you're doing my washing," said Maurice, "I hope you know you're not to use detergent. I'm allergic."

On Friday he did his homework in his room and came down earlier than usual to make his evening cup of tea. Aunt Ada's house was deceptive. It seemed poky but there were still doors he hadn't opened. Like the one between the "breakfast room", where he ate his meals, and the parlour. It was hard to explore because his aunt never seemed to go out, and also she was very quiet on her feet. But now the door was open. Great Aunt Ada was sitting at a big leather covered desk writing something in a notebook. She lifted her head and invited him to share her tea.

"The biscuits, Mary assures me, are quite all right for you."

Maurice poured out carefully into a cup like an eggshell with – of course – roses all over it.

"This is my garden journal," murmured Aunt Ada. "The forsythia should be pruned this week. It is a shrub that should always be pruned vigorously, straight after the flowers. I will telephone Mr Finch. Do you miss a television, Maurice? We could rent one and you could keep it in your room."

She sounded as if she was talking about an exotic pet animal.

"No, I don't miss it," said Maurice. "Thank you."

"I have not heard you coughing in the night. I hope this means that you are being left in peace at the moment."

Maurice smiled bitterly. He knew his great aunt was talking about the asthma. But it was clear by now he was not going to be pestered to death by his loving relatives either. Auntie Sue had turned up on Monday. She was in a tearing hurry, talked about nothing but a crisis at work: told Maurice to be sure and ring if he had any problems, and dashed away. His aunt and uncle had abandoned him, just like his parents. Well, he didn't care. He could learn to live without them all.

"Yes," he said. "I've been left in peace."

Great Aunt went on writing. Maurice decided this must be the scientist's study. It was rather a disappointment. There wasn't any strange Frankensteinish glassware about. There were bookcases with glass doors, but they contained nothing but some fairly modern paperbacks and a pile of old Reader's Digests. It was a lot like sitting in an old-fashioned dentist's waiting room.

"Destroyed," remarked Great Aunt Ada, noticing his curious glances. "The professor destroyed all his books and papers in 1942. I disposed of what remained after his death. But you may look at my album if you wish."

She got up slowly, and fetched a big fat photograph album out of an otherwise empty bookcase. Maurice took it on his knees, and turned over the stiff pages politely. He was flattered. The photographs were very old. He peered at a group of men with beards and moustaches and sideboards running wild over their faces, in front of a background of grey old buildings. There was a forest of names underneath, with James Edward Baxter underlined in red. Great Aunt's professor was a young one in the front row, with hardly any whiskers yet. He tried to read the spidery handwriting, in case there was somebody famous in the picture like Charles Darwin: but there wasn't anyone he'd heard of.

There was some pressed edelweiss, and a sketch of James Edward in front of an alp. Maurice turned the pages gingerly, wondering if he was about to find the secret of the lost invention.

A yellowed cutting from a magazine caught his eye.

Professor Baxter's latest extravagance . . .

Did he become bankrupt? Was that the big secret?

Professor Baxter's latest extravagance, however, goes beyond all bounds. We are unable to understand how a gentleman of such outstanding promise can allow himself to be bamboozled . . . .

Bamboozled's a good word, thought Maurice.

In another moment, he had found out what the extravagance was. He shut the album sharply in embarrassment. He had a horrible feeling he had already told someone – hoping it would get back to Jasmin – that he was living in the former home of a famous scientist.

Great Aunt was looking at him. He felt himself begin to blush.

"You have been reading," she said in her high thin voice, "about the fairies, I suppose."

Maurice coughed and muttered.

"I can see you are surprised. But really there is nothing so very unusual in a belief in those ephemeral creatures. When Professor Baxter was young, many eminently respectable people believed that the forces of Nature could take the form of diminutive and graceful human beings. Dodgson, for instance, the mathematician."

"Lewis Carroll," muttered Maurice. "He wrote *Alice in Wonderland*."

"Exactly. Perfectly sane, you see. And the science of photography being in its infancy, its powers and limitations were still to be discovered. Professor Baxter's only mistake, Maurice, was to continue to express his belief when it had gone out of fashion. He was very stubborn, poor man, in all his researches. That was what led him into trouble."

Maurice fidgeted uneasily. The old lady sighed. After a moment she remarked that it was getting late, and led Maurice out of the study.

At the back of his mind, Maurice had been counting on the mysterious scientist. The Professor Baxter connection made his exile respectable. He had pictured himself discovering the lost formula: something as important as relativity, unrecognised by his ignorant family all these years. And Jasmin, whose parents were doctors, was bound to be impressed by a scientist in the family. The fairies were a serious disappointment.

On Saturday afternoon, alone in Aunt Ada's parlour, he picked up the photograph of James Edward Baxter as young man at Oxford. He looked at the yellow and brownish portrait with resentment. No wonder he ended up "retired" down here. The back of the metal frame bulged, there was something tucked in behind the picture. He twisted the catches and a mottled envelope fell out. It was full of ancient photographs. The science might have been in its infancy, but someone apparently had realised the possibilities of a double exposure. A thin girl with big eyes, in peculiar wispy clothes, was posed standing on tiptoe sniffing at a rose. You could see the rose bush through her . . . .

The backs of the photographs were covered in antique handwriting, giving dates and weather notes for this peculiar kind of bird watching. Poor Professor Baxter, thought Maurice, I wonder who sold him these.

TWO

Maurice began to take over the old cemetery. He regarded it as a refuge from the miseries of life. He wandered about in there after school, delaying his return to Aunt Ada's house so he wouldn't have to face Mary and her stupid questions. Every time she saw him she expressed wild surprise that he hadn't yet flown away to the Gulf; or made some futile comment about his allergies, asking if they hadn't "got well" yet. It got on Maurice's nerves. He was used to being jeered at at school, but it was a bit much to have to endure persecution from a home help.

The housing estates beyond Fairsea had vanished out of Maurice's universe. He couldn't bear to go anywhere near Keymer Drive, and there were no friends to tempt him. What had been a blank wall with a vague fuzz of tree branches over the top, now became his secret world. He formed a close relationship with the poor dead tentacle tree, and spent time working out a beautiful and appropriate inscription for his own gravestone: which he felt might be needed quite soon. Later, in a bitter mood, he decided he would have *The Great Physician came and prescribed rest* . . . Why should he, Maurice, trouble to make people's lives more interesting? Nobody gave him any consideration.

On the whole he was disappointed in the quality of the inscriptions. There was little originality. He started keeping score of the most common ones, and toyed with the idea of drawing a map, on which he would enter discoveries like the shrubbery steps and landmarks like the stone horse. But that plan never developed. He did not want to draw lines around the cemetery. He liked the illusion of mystery: the way he could sometimes persuade himself that he was lost in a jungle, even when he could hear the traffic on both sides.

Deep in the shrubbery he found a headstone with a holly tree growing right round it. There was a slit in the trunk, and the stone disappeared inside as if it was being swallowed. The woman who was turning into a tree was ORA ANNIE ABBEY: *arted this life 25th November 1879 aged 25*. He rubbed moss and ancient dead leaves off the inscription at the bottom. It was only *She has gone to wear an eternal crown* – a fairly common one. But he felt a thrill. Perhaps he was the first person to read those words for a hundred years.

In the dank darkness of the shrubbery steps or wandering among the five star memorials, he brooded over plans to make Jasmin Kapoor notice him. Quite apart from their different cultures, the gulf between third year and second year was so great it was almost impossible to think of a way to cross it. He had once imagined that if he lived in the centre of Brighton instead of pathetically suburban Keymer Drive thousands of opportunities would arise. But the idea was laughable. He never dared venture into the Saturday town centre where a girl might be bumped into. It was no joke starting to wheeze in the middle of an indifferent crowd. He might collapse and get crushed to death before anyone noticed.

What attracted him to Jasmin, apart from her elegant legs, was that she looked as if she felt the same way as he did about Fairsea School. Whenever she wasn't with her particular friends she stared about her with an expression of bleak disdain, wincing visibly at the coarse obscenities, the smells, the lumping charging bodies. Maurice wanted to become her ally against the vile majority. It was as if the two of them had been accidentally locked into a zoo – surrounded by dangerous animals and waiting for the keeper to come and let them out. But no one came.

He hardly ever saw anyone in the cemetery – only the occasional silent figure by a fresh heap of flowers, and he avoided those. Once he spotted Mary the home help bicycling up the path, back to her lodgings on the other side of Fairsea, but he ducked out of sight.

The only person he spoke to was the head gardener: a little old man always dressed in overalls, with a brown and weatherbeaten face. His name was Mr Kidder. He and Maurice became acquainted when he stopped Maurice one day and reminded him he had to leave before the gates were shut. The sudden apparition made Maurice jump. But Mr Kidder bore no resemblance to the old man who had stared and disappeared, on that first day. He didn't think Maurice was weird for hanging about the cemetery. He understood.

"I don't know what I'd do without this place," he said. "I come in here in the mornings and it's my refreshment. It's the quiet and the green things what keeps me going."

Maurice had decided the other old bloke must have been just a stray mourner.

One day Maurice had a bad attack. He was sent out of his Maths lesson and huddled in sickbay creaking like an old lift and sipping water. After a while his condition improved slightly. The nurse had disappeared so he wrote on her pad MAURICE EASTMAN 2M HAS GONE HOME. and took himself off to the cemetery. He sat on a bench just inside the gates, listening to the traffic whipping down Fairsea Hill. The lawn here only had a few collapsed headstones in it, to remind you of its original purpose. A robin hopped about, but flew away when Maurice threw it a few gluten-free crumbs out of his lunch bag.

He knew why he'd had this attack. It was the letter from Ishar; his first. Stupidly, in spite of the evidence, he'd been imagining all this time that they'd be home again in about a fortnight. Not likely! Everything was wonderful, everything was perfect. No reason why Maurice shouldn't come over at half term . . . .

Why couldn't they understand that he didn't want to be uprooted? Life was bad enough without being plunged into a mass of tanned healthy expatriate teenagers, all of them expert scuba divers and no doubt incredibly clever. Anyway, he was English. He didn't want to be foreign. He couldn't understand how his parents could give up on their own country where they were born so easily, so casually.

Maurice counted out his breaths by the second timer on his watch. When they were back to normal, normal for a bad day that is, he got up and wandered on. The sun was warm. The trees were sprouting various tassels and plumes of yellow and greenish pink. Maurice eyed them with grim satisfaction, and inhaled deep deliberate lungfuls of pollen until it occurred to him that no one would know or care if he wheezed to death in here. Then he breathed more cautiously, but he still had no intention of hurrying out of the danger zone.

He couldn't face Mary. *You not sorted out yet? Funny thing, I thought you got all kinds of allowances and accommodations on they Middle East contracts. Don't your Daddy's firm look after you, pay your fare and so on?* He must make sure Aunt Ada understood he couldn't posibly be moved until the end of the summer term. There was still time. The foul Do'an might start to show its nasty side. Perhaps Mum would revolt at being made to wear a black sheet over her head all the time. Any self-respecting woman would.

At the end of the lawn there was a small chapel which was called, according to the sign, the Columbarium. He believed the word meant dovecote in Latin, and in fact the chapel walls were covered in what looked like little doors of pigeons' nesting boxes. But these doors weren't meant to open. Behind each of them there must be an urn containing the remains of someone cremated – it would be impossible to get a whole body into such a small space.

Around the Columbarium there were rosebeds, bare and fibrous now with the roses chopped down to neat green spokes. There was a thick growth of little plastic labels: name tags for the people who had been scattered there. He wondered if the families concerned realised they were being slightly conned. Mrs Maria Edgeworth, dusted down here twenty years ago, was probably spread all over the cemetery by now, and someone else was getting the benefit of her flowers.

Beyond the Columbarium he was in unexplored territory. He could see the spire of the funeral church through the trees directly below him. But he could also see another section of the valley: full of interesting statues and looking pleasantly lonely. He had glimpsed this part from the lower reaches of the red drive, but hadn't been able to find a way into it.

He followed a grass path between banks of turf. The trees grew close on either side, and ivy climbed between them. Lost stones leaned on each other in the tangle: forgotten, long forgotten, with only Maurice to try and read their names . . . . The path ended in a deep grassy hollow. There were two or three graves: a broken celtic cross, a plain headstone and an angel who had dripped into an indistinct stalagmite over years and years of rain. Bushy wild pink valerian half buried the stones, some of it already in flower. There was a fat bee, buzzing earnestly.

Maurice checked out the inscriptions and then sat down, propping himself comfortably against the green wall of the hollow. He could hear the chug chug chug of garden machinery somewhere.

Alas for him who never sees
The stars shine through his cypress trees . . .

He tried idly to remember the next line. He had read the poem elsewhere, on another grass path like this one. It was quite good by the cemetery's standards. Nothing here but two

Great Physicians and a *Voice is Stilled*. The Great Physician forges ahead, thought Maurice. He leaned back, trying to remember the exact totals in his survey of standard epitaphs . . . .

And almost immediately he was somewhere else.

He was lying in a bed. It was a big bed. When he looked up he could see a curtain swaying down above him. It was as if he was lying underneath the belly of a huge red furry animal, because the curtain seemed to be velvet. He turned his head and saw a little fire burning, a real coal fire. On the mantelpiece above it there were two candlesticks, both of them with several branches. He could see silver leaves and petals gleaming on them, and he could hear, somewhere close, a strange noise. A clopping, creaking, rumbling noise. The door of the room opened. A girl came in. She looked about the same age as Maurice, she was wearing a long dress and a cap like a nurse's cap on her head. She carried a huge jug with a cloth folded over it. It was steaming violently. Yuk, thought Maurice. Friar's Balsam. But at the same time, someone else thought: Heigh ho, time to get up. The girl put the jug down somewhere. She crossed the room. There was a rustling sound of curtains being pulled back. Maurice sat up sharply.

He was on the beach. There was a strong smell of brine and tar. He stood with a crowd of other people, his chin buried in the folds of his cravat, glad of his heavy greatcoat and sturdy beaver. Idly he watched a pair of scavenging fishwives trailing sacks behind them as they picked seacoal from the shingle. Wrapped in lace, said somebody. Like a babe in arms. And the cream of it was, there was no duty paid on the lace either. The first man and the person he was talking to both started to laugh . . . . He was in a boat, a little boat crowded with people. It jerked alarmingly. He could see the enormous side of the packet rearing up beside him, slapped by waves of blue green water that spat cold foam at his cheeks . . . .

Maurice struggled. Packets? Beavers? A barrel wrapped up in a christening shawl?

For a moment he felt completely bewildered. He couldn't

understand why he wasn't in bed. Had he been sleepwalking? He stared around. The bee was still buzzing, the cultivator or whatever it was still said chug chug chug. In the distance traffic still faintly hummed on the road. Why on earth should I fall asleep? he thought. He could remember sitting down. He could remember saying to himself a couple of lines he had read on one of the gravestones – in fact "could remember" was too distant. He had been saying that line of poetry about one second ago. Where did falling asleep fit in?

A thought came to him that was very odd *Those weren't my dreams*. They were crystal clear in his mind, the deceptive way dreams are just when you waken from them, but he had the most extraordinary feeling of not owning them. As if he had been there only as a watcher.

He sat looking at the bee on the valerian, feeling quite dizzy. Then he said out loud: "I take drugs. I don't know what I've taken that could affect my mind today, but obviously anti-histamines and asthma drugs can have funny effects. There's nothing to worry about." Then he got up and walked briskly out of the hollow.

He expected the dreams to disappear almost at once, in the peculiar way dreams do. But they didn't. He could remember them as if he'd read them in a book. He couldn't think why this seemed so odd. But it did. He started to head for home: somehow he didn't feel like exploring any more.

On the way through the upper graveyard he passed a van standing open. Two brawny lads beside it were hacking out a pit in the chalk. It was the first time he'd seen grave-diggers actually at work. He'd have liked to stop and watch. But another of the young gardeners was in the open van with the rakes and forks and things, having a break. His hat was pulled over his eyes, his dirty jumpered chest rose and fell peacefully. Maurice glanced nervously at this figure, and passed on. Candlesticks and beavers? he thought. Four poster beds and parcels floating in the sea? He almost wished he dared wake the young man up and ask him.

Maurice had to endure a savage talking-to from his year head, about walking out of sick bay. There could have been a fire, and no one would have known if he was still in the building . . . and so on, and so on. He turned off, and watched the way her glasses bounced on the bridge of her nose as she yelled at him.

Almost immediately after the first letter came another, the answer to Maurice's first one.

Dear Maurice, I'm afraid it's all true. Poor Prof Baxter started life as a brilliant chemist, but he never really got very far, in spite of our family legend. He used to take pictures of fairies in the Master's garden at his Oxford college! I don't know if it was the fairies that finally earned him his early retirement. He had a lot of odd theories about what he called the "chemistry" of the human brain – reincarnation or something. Mum remembers the story but she's forgotten the details. Apparently he was very outspoken. And bitter. He always claimed that his great discoveries were put aside by prejudice and ignorance, and in the end it preyed on his mind and made him quite dotty . . . The reason you haven't heard any of this before is partly because it just didn't come up, but mainly because of your great aunt's feelings. She's had a hard life in some ways, and she's a bit sensitive on the subject of Professor Baxter. But you're old enough now to have some consideration. We didn't keep it from you to start you off on a wild goose chase, that's a silly idea. By the way, you ought to remember he wasn't so "far out" as you might think. Some of the things you take for granted as scientific fact were just wild theories not so long ago. Ask Mr Stewart to tell you about it.

Mr Stewart was a physics teacher. He had made an impression on Maurice's father at a parents' evening once and was ever after referred to as a sort of human encyclopedia, able to answer any possible question on anything.

We have finally found a good flat here, very bare and cool. The building has its own swimming pool! Tabs is missing you, you'll have to come and let her teach you to swim. (I'm exaggerating but she doesn't do too badly for eighteen months.) Mummy doesn't have to wear a black sheet when she goes out, where did you get that idea? This is a pretty liberal state as Islamic countries go. We're both planning to learn Arabic. Not many expats do, but we think it'll be worth the effort after a year or two.

Love from Daddy. And Mum xxx, (this was in his mother's handwriting.)

So that's that, thought Maurice bitterly. His only consolation was that his mother (who couldn't even write half a letter to her lonely son) would soon get sick of such an intellectual struggle, and demand to come home to a place where she at least spoke the language.

That afternoon he went sailing. The lake was brilliant blue as a lake on a holiday poster. Its shores were green and wooded, dotted with little white hotels. Above the woods there were hills, and above the hills were gleaming white mountains. It didn't look like the Lake District. Maurice was sure it wasn't anywhere in Scotland either. The boat bounced over little waves, he felt the wood of the tiller in his hand and heard the sail cracking in the breeze. He was alone but a steamer passed him. Ladies with big hats on leaned at the rail and waved. In real life, Maurice hated boats – even the tame motor launch on the Norfolk broads. He had only once tried to row a dinghy, never mind sail it, and his attempt had been a complete disaster.

He woke in the green hollow and lay for a moment with his eyes closed, savouring the dream. He came straight to this spot now every day after school. The first time he came back, he had been convinced nothing would happen. But it did. By now he knew for sure that if he sat down in a particular angle of the hollow at the end of the overgrown path from the Columbarium, he could close his eyes and be at once in a magical dream more real than real life.

He had thought of various explanations. The most likely was that his asthma drugs combined with a special mixture of cemetery pollens to produce this effect. The strangest was that he was borrowing from someone else asleep at the same time. He also thought the dreams could easily be made up of things he had read or seen on the TV or in films. But never in his life had he dreamed so clearly. He sat up, and tried holding his hands the way he had been holding them on the lake. Awake, he didn't even know which one held the tiller and which the sail's rope.

Whatever it is, he thought, it's wonderful. It was as if he had found a magic carpet made of green grass and little flowers, to carry him away. Perhaps it had been here for years and years: a focus point for unknown natural forces. The gravestones didn't disprove that. It was obvious that no one had visited them for a long time, and anyway people who came to funerals or to arrange flowers weren't likely to sit down and take a nap.

It was getting late. Every time he tried the magic carpet, he managed to keep it going for longer: although he had no control yet over where he went or what he saw. It wouldn't take him to reconnoitre the Do'an, however hard he concentrated. His watch said 17.37 – twenty to six by the clock on the funeral church tower as he passed by. He was wondering if there was a way he could safely ask anyone about the possibility of his drugs causing unusual dreams.

Better not, he decided. Adults would be bound to assume the magic carpet was no better than gluesniffing. It would be impossible to convince them he was making a serious scientific study –. Suddenly Maurice jumped like a rabbit because something went Pzzt! in his ear, as sharp as a stinging insect. He stared around. He was just at the top of the dark steps, at the gap through the wall that separated the rich valley from the shabby part of the graveyard. He rubbed his ear, which felt really stung, and shrugged his shoulders. Someone laughed. When he looked up, he saw there was a girl sitting on the wall, half hidden in the new green leaves of a chestnut tree, her bare brown legs dangling.

"Oh, it's you," he said.

He had seen this girl before. He suspected her of watching

him and following him around, and resented the way she seemed to regard the cemetery as her territory. She was a scruffy looking creature with tangled dark hair always in her eyes and the same bold expression he dreaded in the fierce second-year girls at Fairsea. He believed she bunked off school; but whichever it was it wasn't Fairsea. Because of the hard-faced look he had ignored her spying. She might have friends.

Now she said "Hey, Maurice. D'you want to help me do something funny?"

"How do you know my name?"

The girl ignored that. "Come on –"

She slipped down from the wall and he followed her warily. He was curious, but determined not to be made a fool of. He ducked and hurried after her, keeping watch for an ambush out of the brambles. There wasn't one. Puffed out of breath, he caught up with her in an elder bush.

"You can run pretty fast for a girl," he felt bound to remark, though it wouldn't have been hard for the average five-year-old to outrun Maurice.

"Sssh!"

On the other side of the bush was a little hut that the gardeners used. Beside it, behind a hedge so as not to upset the bereaved, was a vast bin like a builder's skip. It was full of old wreaths and stained ribbons, bits of card and decaying flowers. A short distance away Mr Kidder was working on one of the formal flowerbeds, the purely decorative kind without any plastic name cards. He had dug it over with his motor cultivator and was now planting out primulas.

"See the digger machine," whispered the wild girl. "He's left it all alone. It's getting bored. It wants a bit of attention."

"Go on, Maurice. Do something to distract him."

She pointed to the skip. He was afraid he wouldn't know what to do, but it was extremely simple. He crept behind it, ducked down and threw a wreath into the air. When he saw Mr Kidder get up and come walking towards him looking puzzled, he threw another wreath and ducked out of sight. He heard the sound of the motor cultivator, growling into life. He scurried back to the hedge, bent double. Mr Kidder stopped in his tracks and looked back. The machine, with no one near it, gnashed its jaws and shuddered. Mr Kidder, in great amazement, approached it as if it was a wild animal. It snapped at him. He tried to get behind it – but the cultivator whipped around, growling fiercely. With a quavering, bewildered cry, Mr Kidder turned and ran. He tripped over his own trowel, placed neatly in his path by an unseen hand, and went flying head first into the bin of dead flowers . . . .

Gasping and crowing, Maurice and the strange girl dodged back along the bramble tunnel under the wall, down the shrubbery steps and buried themselves in the deepest rhododendrons.

"His face!"

"The ribbon! The purple ribbon round his ear!"

"I haven't played with him for a long time," said the girl complacently. "He forgets. He'll be peering round the trees again for weeks now."

"But how did you do all that?" demanded Maurice, when he had recovered from the exertion. It had all happened so quickly. It was amazing the way she'd managed to switch the motor on and move that trowel: all without being seen.

She didn't answer, she just laughed in an annoying way.

"I suppose you did it with string," said Maurice, boredly. "I've done tricks like that myself – with string."

This was far from true. But he could not remember when he had laughed so much. He felt slightly ashamed. Poor Mr Kidder, it was pretty stupid after all. Supposing the old gardener had crash landed on something hard – that wouldn't have been very funny. However, it was still wonderful how surprised he had looked, when the cultivator started chewing up his primula bed all on its own. Practical jokes were usually quite out of the question for Maurice. He wouldn't dare, he was far too vulnerable. No one would ever suspect him of being capable of something like that . . . Maurice grinned to himself.

It was dark and dusty inside the tangle of rhododendrons, with a tilted armless angel for company. The girl sat quietly, without any worry about her clothes, with a calm sweet look on her face: so calm and sweet it was hard to believe what she'd just been doing. He decided he was glad she didn't go to Fairsea. She was definitely the kind who never got herself into trouble. She would lead you into things and dump you there: he knew the sort.

"How did you know my name?"

"Oh, I just heard," she said. "You've come to live with your great aunt, haven't you. Why shouldn't I know about it?"

"Well, what's yours?"

"Moth."

It must be a joke, unless she liked being called by her second name, like a boy at boarding school. She wants me to say "that's not a name," he thought. Well, I'm not going to humour her. In the distance they heard the van driving by.

"We've waited long enough," said Moth. "Let's creep out and make sure they've all gone."

The hut was quiet. They slipped down to the end of the path and saw the garage by the cemetery office shut and padlocked.

"Oh, no!" cried Maurice.

It was past six o'clock and the gates were shut.

There was someone in the office still, the door was open.

"I'll have to go and ask Mr Kidder to let us out."

He started forward. But the girl stopped him.

"You'd better not, Maurice. He doesn't think you played that trick. He thinks you're a nice boy. But what if he knows you were hanging around here? He might get suspicious."

Maurice stared at her. Moth grinned maliciously, showing very white teeth. The ones in the corners of her mouth were unusually pointed, giving her a wicked look. He felt challenged. He knew nothing would please her better than to see him start to panic. He did not point out that the funny business with the cultivator had been all her idea.

"So what?" he remarked coolly. "I don't care what he thinks."

"But I know where you can get out. Miss Amelia Forbes will help us. Or the Colonel, only I think they've moved him."

"What do you mean? What Colonel?"

Moth skipped away. It was still daylight but the graveyard felt slightly different, as if the closing of the gates had changed something in the atmosphere. Moth ran and jumped with no regard at all for the people lying quietly underfoot and Maurice came hopping after her occasionally muttering "excuse me".

She stopped on a minor path, close under the outer wall but out of sight of the office.

"Here's the Colonel. But they have moved him."

"What on earth are you talking about?"

"The bench, of course. Look –"

It was a heavy grey oak bench like the one he had found up on the lawn. Moth was pointing to a little metal plaque screwed onto its back:

In loving memory of Colonel Herbert Waldon
*   1860–1936 "At Ease"*

"The Colonel, you see."

On the other side of this wall was great aunt's garden, and the gardens of other houses in her terrace. But it was far too high. Impossible for Maurice.

"We'd better try Miss Amelia. Hurry up."

She went racing off again, skirting the office widely, and Maurice followed, over the flowery turf. The blue haze of evening had begun to gather, and birds were singing loudly.

"Hurry, hurry –"

Miss Amelia Forbes was at the other end of the same path, conveniently placed up against the wall. Her inscription, under the "in memory of" and the dates, was *A dear friend*.

Moth patted the grey oak arm cheerfully. "Miss Amelia is very reliable."

"Who does the bench on the lawn belong to?" asked Maurice curiously. "The one near Fairsea gate?"

"Oh, that's Felicia May Dalton. A beloved wife and mother. She can be a little odd. You shouldn't hang around near her after the gates have closed."

The ground had sloped up and the wall was much lower here. Dubiously Maurice climbed on to the back of the bench and peered over, but even he couldn't say it was a long way down. In a moment he stood on the verge of the allotments that began where the houses ended on great aunt's hill. He looked back down at Moth.

"Hadn't you better go and fetch your shoes?" he suggested. "You can't walk down the streets like that."

"Oh, I'm not coming out" she said. "I've got better things to do. Go on, Maurice. Your great aunt will be wondering."

Three

One dream experience was rather frightening. It began in a railway station: a dark and cavernous place. Everything seemed larger than lifesize, including the massive iron pillars and arches. The ticket windows looked like parts of an antique space ship. The trains were steam trains – enormous and clumsy, heaving themselves along in hissing clouds of grey fog. Then the station disappeared and he saw people walking on a sea shore, on a wide road. It was like a holiday crowd but it must be the middle of winter wherever it was, because everyone was wrapped up in cloaks and coats and shawls, and Maurice felt pretty cold. There was no tarmac on the road, it was just sand and dirt. It opened up into a broad long dirty space, with a few trees growing in it and houses or maybe hotels around the edges.

The scene changed to a room inside a house. It was dark and poky. Maurice sat in a bed and examined the unusual furniture – what he could see of it. Then he realised that there was a storm going on outside. The wind howled, the waves roared, rain rattled against the window. He got up and went to look out. For a moment the lightning lit up a long line of white houses, and he saw a strange construction like half a suspension bridge, like loops of giant ribbons. The sky went black again. Maurice began to cry. He knew the house was going to blow down. He had heard his Mama saying it was only made out of boards .... In the darkness there came a rending, terrible crashing thunder ....

Maurice screamed, and woke up in the green hollow. That wasn't nice, he muttered.

But where was that place? He'd never seen anything like it. The people in the railway station were filthy. He still felt as if his lungs must be covered in a black film from breathing that sooty steam. Considering that the streets weren't even paved, he decided he must have been transported to somewhere in the Third World. But nowhere in the Third World would be cold like that. Perhaps it was Russia. There might well be places in Russia where they still had steam trains. Or China? Thinking hard, he seemed to remember seeing a kind of rickshaw in the crowd on the broad dirt track, pulled by an animal. What sort of animal? Maybe it was a llama. Maybe he'd just been visiting some primitive city high up in the Andes.

But he hadn't been Maurice. He'd been a little child. That was obvious, from everything looking so big, and the way the person in the dream felt about a mere thunderstorm. He was slightly worried by this. The "dream experiences", as he called them, hadn't turned him into a different person before. Except for the very first time when he didn't know what was happening, they had been like a highly superior video game with super-realistic effects. He decided he must have accidentally given himself an overdose. Spring was progressing, the pollen count was rising: maybe that was it. I don't want to wake up with the mind of a toddler, he thought. Perhaps I won't come back for a day or two. But of course he did.

On the way to the yellow stone gates at great aunt's end of the cemetery he noticed something odd. A thin spidery figure creeping along, in a coat that looked too big for her. It was Aunt Ada herself. She was carrying a little bunch of flowers. Maurice was amazed. He had never seen her on the street before. Without thinking, he ducked behind the gardeners' hut. He had the strangest idea she must be spying on him. It was nonsense, of course. But when he joined her for the usual evening cup of tea, he noticed that she didn't mention where she'd been.

Later that week 2M went into town for a history lesson. They took the bus to the seafront and walked along the promenade. Carole Verne, Andrew Bolt and various other assorted enthusiasts clustered round Ms Lycett the history teacher. There was a parent too: Carole Verne's father. Apparently he was wildly interested in local history. Ms Lycett had made them all thank him for helping to organise this trip. Maurice thought the man must be mad. The dregs of 2M trailed behind, surreptitiously bashing each other with their clipboards. Maurice was up with the enthusiasts, for safety: and also because he saw a chance to get some information. It was a cold gloomy day, safely between Easter and Whitsun so they had the front more or less to themselves.

"Ms Lycett," asked Maurice, carefully pronouncing the Miz to put her in a good mood, "do you know anything about dreams?"

"What kind of dreams? Do you mean ambitions, or the dreams you have when you're asleep?"

"Oh, asleep. I mean scientifically. Could you – has anyone ever heard of anyone dreaming the same dream as someone else?"

He spoke as casually as he could.

Ms Lycett answered thoughtfully, "Well, there are people who are quite convinced it happens. A friend of mine was ill in Switzerland once – she was an au pair – and her mother rang her up because she'd dreamed there was something wrong."

"That's not exactly what I meant –"

He stopped, wondering how to explain without giving anything away. But Ms Lycett now had a gleam in her eye.

"I haven't had a chance to talk to you for a while, Maurice. How is life at your auntie's?"

"Oh, it's all right."

She had that keen expression – a teacher on the trail of a problem child. On occasions like this he wished the school had never heard of his asthma. He ought to just go and lock himself in a toilet when his lungs started to seize up. Pretend to be bunking off whenever he had an allergy, instead of plastering their desks with sicknotes. He thought resentfully if he was one of the really criminal types they'd be afraid of him and leave him alone.

"It must be upsetting, having your parents so far away. I suppose that would give anyone bad dreams."

Maurice realised a sensible scientific conversation was impossible.

"Oh, I don't mind," he said sarcastically. "It doesn't bother me at all. I don't care if I never see them again, really."

He walked on his own after that, dumbly accepting a new form of torture. They went down a ramp to the hard above the shingle, where booths under the promenade were selling fish and chips and hamburgers and candyfloss. Alec Verne told them Brighton used to be called "Brighthelmstone", but it was still pronounced Brighton even then. The original channel ferry used to leave from this very beach. He talked about fishwives carrying Brighton fishermens' catch along the Jugg's Road, over the downs to Lewes. Later on, smugglers used that old track to transport lace and brandy from France that had not paid any import duty . . . .

Maurice wasn't listening. He hadn't the slightest idea what was supposed to be happening today. He thought it was a stupid trick to bring a wild pack of Fairsea animals down to the sea front, supposing you had to take them anywhere. If he was unemployed like Mr Verne, he was sure he could have found something better to do. Ms Lycett reminded the class it was forbidden to buy or eat junk food in school time, but John Drummond and Jason Trevor bought little fried doughnuts rolled in sugar and strolled at the back, munching.

The ordinary boy, Ghengis's brother, invited Maurice to

read some dirty postcards with him. Maurice declined, and followed the others under the pier, where the sea roared dismally and rushed, horribly dark green, around rusty pillars. He gazed at it in despair. It was all his parents' fault, going off to the Persian Gulf and leaving him in this zoo.

Soon the ordinary boy was lost in the distance, carefully twirling a rack of fat pink men and improbable looking blonde girls with enormous busts. He had a reading age of about six, so it was going to take him all afternoon. No one noticed that he'd been left behind. Maurice huddled his coat around him. The other boys were wearing parkas or bulging padded anoraks. Maurice forgot that he had demanded an overcoat, considering it more sophisticated and adult; and blamed his mother for making him different. Fresh air for the lunatics, he thought. Once around the exercise yard.

"Bit of a joke isn't it," said Carole Verne.

"Huh?"

"But it keeps my Dad happy. Have you seen all the project stuff in the library? He's got Andrew and me and Jasmin Kapoor up there after school, making bits of old pier out of cardboard . . . ."

Maurice suddenly came to life.

"*Jasmin?*"

"You know – the coloured girl. Funny isn't it. You wouldn't think she'd be interested in English things."

Up ahead, Mr Verne had stopped and Ms Lycett was herding stragglers. Maurice shot away from Carole, not even pausing to sneer at her racist attitude. Mr Verne was telling his fans that in Victorian times the high season would have been over now, as it was considered healthiest to come to the seaside in winter. Nobody ever sunbathed, they would have thought that a mad idea.

"You can imagine the crowds strolling along where the Old Steine is now. In those days there was no asphalt. They laid down oak bark and sawdust to absorb the horses' droppings."

"Euergh–"

Maurice had a vague feeling of something connecting in the back of his mind. But nothing could have been further from his thoughts than the "dream experiences" just then. He wanted to know about this "project" in the library. It was vitally important, a way to get near Jasmin, across the massive barriers of age and culture. Ms Lycett was forcing John Drummond to throw away the rest of his doughnuts. 2M huddled on the undercliff walk, halfway to the Marina. Maurice was oblivious of everything but the thought of Jasmin. A shared hobby – why had he never thought of that before?

Then he saw the plaque on the undercliff wall: an engraving of a one-ended suspension bridge. Loops of steel ribbon reached out over the seawater. It looked oddly familiar.

"On this very spot stood Brighton's first pier," said Ms Lycett dramatically, having dealt with John. "It was opened in 1823, and decorated for the reception with sixteen thousand variegated lamps."

The enthusiastic part of 2M peered at its worksheets, and noted the amazing amounts of cast iron etc which had gone into the Chain Pier; its great success with visitors.

"It was finally destroyed in a great storm in December 1896."

"It must have been quite a storm," murmured someone respectfully.

The vague feeling at the back of Maurice's mind suddenly became clear.

The waves rose, black as black: huge and crushing –

The ordinary boy came hurrying up. His face, red from running, took on a look of alarm.

"Hey, Maurice, are you all right? Miss – look at Maurice!"

Maurice groaned loudly. He couldn't help it.

I was there, I was there, he wanted to shout. But he couldn't shout anything because he couldn't get his breath.

Suddenly the ordinary boy grabbed him by the waist from behind and heaved. He was trying to carry out a First Aid trick he had seen on television, used on the victims of choking.

"Hey, stop that," shouted Ms Lycett, thinking it was a fight. Passers by suddenly appeared from nowhere, and exclaimed in disgust.

But Maurice couldn't stop. He could hear the awful noises he was making but he couldn't do anything to control them. He collapsed against the wall grabbed his knees and heaved and heaved, while Ms Lycett bent over him with an expression of exasperation and dismay, and Mr Verne herded up the others and calmed the bystanders. *It's the past*, he thought dizzily. *The dreams, it's the past. I've been in the past.* Then he couldn't think of anything at all except breathing, or rather trying to breathe and not succeeding.

Mr Verne wanted to call an ambulance, but Ms Lycett briskly took charge and sent Carole to call a taxi. Eventually Maurice was helped up to the upper promenade, where he crouched in a shelter wheezing horribly, feeling as if a strait-jacket was strapped round his ribs. 2M gaped at him. They still found Maurice Eastman's fits impressive. He heard Ms Lycett murmur to Mr Verne, "He's very easily upset, I'm afraid".

"Perhaps he should be at a special school," whispered Carole's father.

Maurice didn't care. He stayed huddled like a toad until the taxi driver arrived, and lifted him solicitously into the car. Mr Verne had to travel back with him, leaving Ms Lycett and 2M to catch the bus. It was the kind of miserable humiliation Maurice had endured all his life. But this time it meant nothing at all. He even went on groaning longer than he had to, because it gave him peace to think.

Now he could see the ladies on that steamer in the lake, with their long and trailing dresses. And all the other visions: crinolines and carriages with horses. And the trains in the Chain Pier dream. Why had he not realised? Because it was so natural, that was why. Inside a dream experience he never caught himself wondering "where's the electric light switch?" It was different from any time travelling he had ever seen or read about. It was like becoming someone in history, with their thoughts and their eyes; and still being Maurice at the same time. But of course it's different, he told himself. It's real.

He spent the next morning in bed, whistling like a kettle and drinking pints of water. In the afternoon he told Aunt Ada he felt he needed some fresh air, but he wasn't well enough for school. She accepted this placidly. He believed she could hardly tell the difference between schooldays and weekends.

He went straight to his magic carpet, quite certain it wasn't going to work, and he was just making a fool of himself.

Alas for him who never sees
The stars shine through his cypress trees . . .

He always repeated those lines in his head, though he wasn't sure what difference it made, because of the first time.

He was in a street. It was a wide street, quite normal and everyday; lined with shops. There was traffic going by, people going in and out of doorways. Maurice looked in shop windows and caught some thoughts running along beside his own. Sausages and a new kind of voile and whether cook had been listening about the plum jam – Well, this is just ordinary, thought Maurice, acutely disappointed. A car came round the corner. Everyone in the street was instantly paralysed, as if a spaceship had landed, pouring out stun rays. And Maurice had the extraordinary privilege of seeing a motor-car, with its thin spider-spoked wheels and goggle eyes, as a new animal . . . The common or garden street somersaulted. He saw women with bustles, men in fantastic tall hats, horse carriages of all kinds clomping and clanking with an amazing amount of noise and smell. Who invented pollution and traffic jams? . . . The date, he thought excitedly. The date! He tried to look up and down the street, searching for a newsagent. But just as in a real dream he was helpless. He couldn't make his own head turn. Bang! The motor-car backfired and Maurice started violently, with that falling-off-a-cliff feeling.

"Bother."

He sat up, frowning. Someone laughed. He looked round

and saw the girl called Moth sitting on the edge of the hollow peering down at him, her face framed in a tangle of greenery.

"What are you doing there?" he asked sharply.

"I've been watching you." She was still watching, with a knowing expression that Maurice didn't like. "You ought to be careful, Maurice. It isn't safe to pick the flowers that grow in King Death's Garden. You'll get into trouble."

"What d'you mean – "King Death's Garden"?"

"This place, of course. It's all Death's Garden." She pointed, smiling, at the blurred angel and the broken celtic cross.

He felt quite strange for a moment. He had almost forgotten, since his scientific experiences began, that this was a graveyard.

"I don't know what you're talking about. I don't pick flowers. I'm not a stupid girl."

Moth laughed, and then looked solemn. "Oh, Maurice. *You do know*."

Maurice stared at her. Then he said angrily, "Why don't you just clear off. And mind your own business."

But without waiting for her to go, he got up and marched away himself. Moth laughed again. It was the end of April, the wallflowers that grew by the broken cross were in full bloom. She picked a spray of sweet tawny flowers, tucked it in her hair, and vanished into the trees.

Alec Verne was delighted to have a new recruit, although rather worried in case Maurice should have another fit. The library history project had been started by a Writer in Residence. She was long gone, but Mr Verne kept it going. Jasmin Kapoor was very faithful too. She had a talent for technical drawing and model making.

Everything seemed to fall into place. He went into the library after school, and was readily accepted by the group of adults and schoolchildren. Maurice was quite good at art. He had already made some drawings of his "dream experiences".

He brought them in and gave them to Mr Verne ("call me Alec –") – without saying anything about magic carpets, of course. It would be useful to have an expert opinion.

And Jasmin smiled at him. Jasmin talked to him. She was interested in what he had to say about the cemetery, though she laughed at the idea that she might like to explore it herself. He had more to tell – but not in public.

On Friday after school he saw her making off on her own towards the racecourse. He knew now this was a history project day, when the dark car wouldn't turn up for another hour. It seemed only natural to follow her. He felt almost as if he'd been invited.

He followed her slim dark figure across the open grass by the allotments, over the road and through the concrete tunnel that went under the course, coming out on common ground where there was a market on bank holidays. She wore a dark blue skirt and dark blue leggings. Maurice had never even seen her ankles. The ordinary boy reported (he claimed to have contacts in the girls' changing rooms) that Jasmin's legs were actually hairy, but Maurice didn't believe it.

He came out of the tunnel, blinking into daylight and saw Jasmin leaning against a fence. Beside her was Aziz the fourth year movie star. They weren't actually kissing but it was a fairly compromising position. Maurice was so disappointed he must have groaned out loud. Deceitful girl! She never even looked at Aziz in school.

Jasmin saw Maurice. She went completely rigid. Her face changed in an instant from its usual olive tawny colour to a horrible greenish yellow.

"Well – I'll be off then," said Aziz the movie star, after an awkward silence.

Maurice, who had expected Aziz to belt him one, if anything, was amazed to see his rival beating a swift retreat.

"Sorry," he said to greenish Jasmin. "I didn't mean to interrupt. I was just passing."

Her nostrils were so pinched they turned white at the edges.

"You little sneak," she hissed. "You devil! If you tell anyone I'll kill you."

"I was just –"

"You little pig. Filthy leprous little brute. You come near me again with your rashes and your stupid put-on retching noises and I'll report you to the head . . . ."

He would have been afraid of physical violence if her expression hadn't been so utterly disgusted. It was obvious she wouldn't touch him with gloves and a mask. She rushed past him into the tunnel, and he was left gasping, with a last image of her light brown eyes glaring into his: a savage hissing voice. "If you tell anyone about me and Aziz I'll kill you!"

He was so outraged then he didn't even feel the wounding insults. He couldn't help walking past her and her boyfriend. It was a public place. If Jasmin Kapoor had ever had asthma the way he did she'd know there was nothing "put-on" about it. How would she like it if he started calling her a wog?

But in his bedroom at Aunt Ada's, the shock wore off and he began to feel the pain. So that was what Jasmin Kapoor thought of Maurice Eastman. A filthy leprous little brute.

"So now I know," he muttered.

He wished he was in the Do'an. He wished he was dead.

He looked at the photographs of his family: bursting with health and happiness. He took out an airmail form and started to write vindictively. Dear Mother, Dad and Tabitha. I hope there aren't any earthquakes. I have heard that they are quite common around Ishar, generally with severe casualties . . . .

Jasmin lay in wait for him in the library forecourt on Monday.

"Hey, Maurice, I'm sorry I said that about your asthma. I shouldn't have. You can't help it."

Maurice shrugged his shoulders. He noticed she didn't apologise for the other things she'd said.

"But you won't tell, will you?"

"What's there to tell?" asked Maurice. He really couldn't see that he had any material for blackmail.

Jasmin's eyes darkened. "You don't know my parents," she said grimly.

For a moment he felt a twinge of sympathy, wondering if his beautiful ex-idol was secretly a battered child. But he remembered that he had turned his back on the world, so he simply shrugged his shoulders again and walked away.

In King Death's Garden the cherry trees were clotted thick with pink and white flowers, the petals dripping on to the ground beneath like melted ice cream. Maurice and Moth the wild girl came quietly on to the lawn by the Fairsea gate and watched two grey squirrels sitting in the daisies beside Felicia May Dalton's bench.

"They're just rats," whispered Maurice. "They've driven out the red ones."

"What do I care?" said Moth. "They're pretty things."

The squirrels skipped away at a leisurely pace with their tails floating behind them, not at all worried about Moth and Maurice or the growling traffic. They knew they were in sanctuary.

Moth's hair was never brushed. Her clothes were brightly coloured but there was always something ragged and unfinished about them, as if they were homemade by somebody inspired but uncaring who picked things up and dropped them casually. When he first met her he thought she had just been on her Easter holidays abroad and got a suntan, but later he changed his mind. He found her out of doors in all weather just in her dress: she seemed quite used to being drenched and cold. Maurice remembered his own plans to become the wild boy of Keymer Drive, and realised with grudging admiration that he could never have survived the kind of life Moth was living.

She seemed to turn up more and more now he had turned his back on the world. He tried to find out more about her, but failed completely. He couldn't follow her home when she refused steadfastly to leave the cemetery while he was around. He didn't know which school she went to: and anyway as far as he could work out she was never there. He had a theory for a while that her parents were hippies, and she lived in a commune where they practised free love and lived on lentils.

But he decided the truth was probably less romantic. Near the top of great aunt's hill, just below the allotments, there was a street of dark little houses with junk in the front gardens. There were windows boarded up with cardboard, and occasionally a burned out car might be seen by the kerb. Most likely that was where Moth belonged. He resolved to ask her no more questions. She was like him, an outcast. She was better off lurking in the cemetery, he was certain, than she would be in care.

They watched thrushes smashing snail shells, they collected caterpillars and teased spiders. Nothing was too trivial to amuse Moth. They watched the cemetery's resident tomcat stalking a fieldmouse between two weeping angels. Maurice winced at the last soft clever pounce, but Moth was a realist. She laughed and clapped her hands. "Oh! – Well played, sir!"

She used some odd expressions – "Jolly good show" was another one – as if she'd been reading Sherlock Holmes. But she must have picked them up from the TV, it was hard to imagine her with a book in her hand.

One day she showed him where a pair of bluetits were nesting in a hole in the trunk of a sycamore tree by the shrubbery steps. Rain poured down, but Maurice forgot to worry about his chest. The two tiny birds shot in and out of their hole, scruffy and bedraggled in the heavy shower.

"They can't stop for a minute," said Moth. "This is their second try. They've got twelve in there alive. They're very ugly."

"Twelve? How do you know?"

"Easy. I counted."

"Oh, very funny. Didn't you find it a bit dark in that hole?"

"Oh yes. And smelly. I kept stepping in bird dirt."

She had a very childish sense of humour. The dress was blue today. It looked fit for a jumble sale like all her others.

"Don't you ever go to school, Moth?"

"Not me. I've got better things to do."

Maurice remembered his resolution, and didn't ask any more.

"I think the rain's stopped" he remarked. "Er – I'm going for a walk."

He didn't mind playing Moth's childish games, but of course that wasn't the real reason he came to the cemetery.

Moth giggled. She grubbed in her pocket and produced what looked like a sprig of purple clover: rather squashed and faded.

"Here," she said. "It's for you."

"What is it?"

"That's self-heal Maurice. It's better for you than those other flowers."

"Stupid girl." He threw the little thing away, and set off for the Columbarium path and another magic journey.

But though she teased, Moth never threatened to interfere in Maurice's private affairs. Other people were not so good at minding their own business. However unfriendly he was to Mary the home help she just wouldn't leave him alone.

Several times she invited him to come and see her at her bedsit, because it must be lonely work living with the old lady: a suggestion that Maurice viewed with horrified amazement. Often she was still at great aunt's house when he came in from school (or rather from King Death's Garden). She sat with him in the breakfast room while he ate his tea, her big arms folded on the table top, watching him with relentless friendly interest.

"It's good you've come here to stay with the old lady," she said. "I see a difference in her."

"Um," said Maurice. He didn't. Aunt Ada was just as hardly there as ever.

"No, but you ought to spend some time here anyway. Your mother don't have her parents any more, it's right you know what family she have left."

"Your mother doesn't have her parents," Maurice corrected her coldly – and Mary shouted with laughter.

"We not talking about my mother, mister schoolteacher."

She told him about her other "cases". She told him about her lodgings – he heard the continuing saga of the people upstairs and the people downstairs and the landlady who was "Frankly, a pig. Though I say it to a child." Once when she got really carried away she started to tell him the story of her life.

"Of course I didn't come here to be a home help. When I came here from my own country I had a scholarship. I am a sculptress, originally –"

Maurice glanced at her, with her pudgy washing up hands and bulging nylon overall, and barely hid a smile.

"Oh, really?"

Mary got up suddenly and began to bustle about. She looked angry and ashamed. But it served her right, thought Maurice, for making up stories.

Worst of all, she kept remarking in wonderment at the length of time it took him to walk home from school. How many times did he have to sit down on the way? Did the doctor know he was so short of breath? If Maurice had had nothing to hide he would quite cheerfully have told her that he just happened to like graveyards. But he didn't want anyone to know about the magic carpet until he had worked things out on a proper scientific basis.

She came into his room on a Saturday. He had expressly told her that he didn't want his room tidied but she took no notice.

"What you doing, Maurice?"

"It's a kind of project."

He was reading several books at once. One called *Memories, Dreams, Reflections* proved totally impractical: but he had a medical dictionary, a book about people floating in tanks in California, and another on ley lines. Somewhere in here was the answer to the mystery . . .

"For school work?"

"Sort of."

There was something about Mary that made him too nervous to tell a decent lie.

"I think I might send it to my parents. They'd be interested."

Mary picked up his private photographs that had come with the last Do'an letter.

"You think so? Funny thing, they look to me more of an out of doors type."

Maurice covered his work with his arm. He was trying to write a scientific description of one of the dream experiences. He gave Mary a threatening look, which she ignored.

"You think they don't like you enough, huh? I know that. You say it often enough without saying it."

He pretended not to hear. He was outraged. How dare she! She was a home help, not a social worker.

Mary heaved a sigh. She stood at the window, pushed aside the lace and peered out thoughtfully.

"Maurice – I don't see any harm in you going to visit the cemetery. What the point of having a garden of remembrance if nobody ever goes there and remembers, whether they connected with anybody buried or not. But it don't make sense, Maurice, for you to stay in there every day so long . . ."

Maurice went on writing. But suddenly he said in a cold voice.

"If you're supposed to be a sculptress, how come you're working as a home help?"

Mary let the curtain drop.

"I have a bad back" she said at last with dignity. "I told you that. I had to give it up because of my bad back."

"If you've got a bad back, how come you're working as a home help? What would you do if my great aunt fell down or something? Does the Council know you've got a bad back?"

Mary stared at him a full minute with no expression on her face at all.

"I got work to do," she said, and stalked out of the room. Maurice laughed, so that she could hear him.

Four

Maurice was too proud to give up the history project after his horrible experience with Jasmin. He was afraid Carole Verne or Andrew would guess why he'd joined up and what had happened. Jasmin clearly felt the same: she talked to him just as before. But he knew it was false. He could still hear her saying *"filthy leprous little brute"*

He didn't care. She'd be sorry, really sorry, if she knew what she'd missed by insulting him. Just across the road he had something far more exciting than any of these pathetic history fans could possibly imagine.

He sent his scientific description of a dream experience to Caltec. He was so suspicious of Mary he hid the letter in his briefcase and took it off into town to post it. She gossiped with the woman at the Post Office at the bottom of the hill. He had heard her: he was sure it was illegal. *What you writing to a Institute of Technology for, Maurice? You only a schoolboy. Funny thing – I didn't know you had any family in California . . . .*

He smuggled valerian, wallflower and other sprigs of vegetation from what he had learned to call the phenomenon location, and kept them in a jar hidden under his bed. Mary kicked the jar over. She was amazed and horrified that he should be keeping pollen in his room "right alongside all that asthma medicine!" So she said. Maurice believed she had destroyed his experiment deliberately.

The home help was obviously a natural busybody, but he was becoming convinced there was more to it than that. There was a distinctly shifty look in Mary's eye when she tried to tell him not to visit the cemetery. And when he remarked that Aunt Ada was the one to tell him what to do, if anyone, Mary definitely took fright. She told him he mustn't bother his auntie about things like that.

Why not? Maurice remembered his father's letter, and felt excited. Professor Baxter had discovered something, while he was living in this house. Something so weird that nobody took him seriously, and he burned his papers in despair. What if that something had been time travel? He became convinced that Aunt Ada knew more than she was telling. Clearly she had shown him that album, with the nonsense about fairies, just to put him off the scent.

He wanted to interrogate her, but that wasn't so easy. She moved around like a cross between a cat and a cobweb. And though she looked so spidery she had her own kind of power. Without saying a word she had established that her room upstairs and the study downstairs were sacred territory, where Maurice could not enter without invitation. Even outside those doors it was as if she lived in another dimension, in the world of forty years ago; thinly showing through into modern times. Sometimes she passed Maurice on the stairs and smiled at him so politely he was sure she didn't remember his name.

But his chance came. On Spring Bank Holiday Monday he declined an invitation from Aunt Sue and Uncle Tom, to go with the cousins to a safari park. Instead he took his great aunt down to the sea. He had been asking her "if there was anything he could do" whenever their paths crossed. He had been thinking more in terms of winding wool, or unscrewing tight lids off jars. He was rather daunted by the prospect of being in charge of an eighty-year-old lady on the streets of bank holiday

Brighton, but it couldn't be helped. Her arthritis was playing up, and the time it took to walk her down to the bus stop was incredible.

Luckily she didn't want to walk any more once they got to the front. He settled her in a shelter that still had all the glass in its three walls, to watch the world go by.

"This is a great treat," said Aunt Ada. "I want no more than this. I like the role of a spectator, don't you, Maurice?" Maurice was so keyed up that this seemed like a very strong hint.

"Wouldn't Mary bring you?" he asked, playing it cool.

Aunt Ada sighed. "Willingly, of course. But Mary is rather a lively companion. A little too much for quiet people sometimes."

They relapsed into silence. It was a beautiful day. The sky was cloudless, the Channel reflected it with a warm bright blue. It seemed as if, if you dived into that water you would find brightly coloured fishes flickering over red and purple coral. It was hard to imagine murk and grimy pebbles.

Trails of foreign students loped past, playing gibbons along the railings and yelling at each other in French and German: holidaymakers in their smartest clothes with children eating chips and candyfloss hurried down to the beach. Two fierce-looking skinhead youths were lying in wait, with a couple of small monkeys dressed up – trying to intimidate people into having their pictures taken. The monkeys showed their teeth viciously at the reluctant customers. Up from the pebble strand came the rush of waves and the yells of children and the blaring of pop music, all merged into one confused seaside roar.

"I suppose you miss your professor," suggested Maurice cunningly.

"After forty years? Not really, Maurice. Although he was a great and good friend to me. And I won't hear a word against him," she added, pursing her lips.

This was just the entry Maurice had been hoping for.

58

"But people did say things about him, didn't they?"

"They did. They disliked – our neighbours disliked his habit of walking alone in the lovely garden beyond my garden wall."

The seaside roared by. Maurice waited with bated breath.

"But he wasn't alone, you see," murmured Aunt Ada. "He had a faithful companion, someone who kept him young. That was what he always used to tell me. Who shared wonders with him – even in the middle of the bustling town . . . ."

Maurice started. Here was something he had not expected. But of course, it was quite likely the prof would have a lab assistant.

"This – er, companion. Would he be still alive?"

Aunt Ada turned to him with a puzzled look. "Alive? Oh, I see. No, Maurice. I wasn't referring to a human companion. He had the company we always have in lovely lonely places, if we have eyes to see."

She meant Nature, or something like that. The trouble with eighty-year-old people, thought Maurice, is that because you expect them to be nutty, everything they say starts sounding weird.

Next to them on the bench a woman had settled with a little girl in tow and a baby in a pushchair. The little girl was kicking up a fuss because she couldn't have her crisps until she'd eaten her sandwich. Maurice shuddered. If it wasn't for the interrogation, nothing would have induced him to visit the seafront today. Any moment now a pack of bikers would probably arrive and start throwing petrol bombs. He imagined Aunt Ada would just carry on sitting there enjoying the role of a spectator.

"Did he ever find anything in there? Anything – odd? Something old, that was there before the cemetery?"

She smiled at him. "Everywhere is old, Maurice. You are old yourself. We all come from the past. The stones Mr Finch digs up in my flowerbeds and throws away are ancient and mysterious, though they may not bear the imprint of fossil life. The past is all round you, living and growing. Even the flowers, that are new every spring and last for a day, are old, very old. *Oh, no man knows, through what wild centuries roves back the rose . . . .".*

This last, Maurice realised, was a quotation.

"Poor Professor Baxter. They all turned against him in the end. But I was never disturbed. I saw no reason to be frightened of mere shadows. Besides, I owed him a great deal. And so I have always done my best."

"Your best?"

The faded blue eyes suddenly looked sharp and intelligent, in spite of the crooked glasses and sticking plaster.

"To respect his memory, Maurice."

That was it. He tried to get her talking again, but there was nothing doing. She folded her hands placidly over her fat old lady's handbag, beamed at the horrible little girl and settled back to gaze in a peaceful stupor at the crowds and the sea.

Maurice walked down to the Palace Pier, where coaches rolled up and spilled out hordes of Japanese and Swedes and people from the Midlands. The monkey youths were lurking by the candyfloss stall. Skateboards and rollerskates crashed on the broad tarmac, seagulls screamed and flashed their wings. He stood in the middle of it all like a ghost, thinking of King Death's Garden. There was no doubt. Professor Baxter had found something in the cemetery. It must, it simply must, be the same thing that Maurice had found. He wasn't taken in by Aunt Ada's semi-senile act. He was pretty sure she knew exactly what he was trying to get out of her. She was determined to keep the secret. He would have to persuade her that Professor Baxter wouldn't be called "eccentric" now. Not if it could be proved that his discovery was real. People used to think Einstein was eccentric. And Isaac Newton.

He had tried "asking Mr Stewart" as his father had advised. But Mr Stewart was only sarcastic. Unfortunately Maurice wasn't one of the star pupils in the physics lab, or any kind of lab. Stewpot ought to know that one great discovery was worth ten million stupid school experiments. But he didn't. He would have to be tackled later, when Maurice had collected more evidence.

Down on the pebbles a little girl was having her shoes and socks put back on and roaring furiously. She escaped and ran off, throwing handfuls of shingle at her pursuers. Maurice thought he recognised the bull-like roar. It was Ghengis, the ordinary boy's hyperactive little sister. Innocent bystanders winced and wiped pebbles off their necks: Ghengis's mother and father and the ordinary boy crept up on her like commandos.

Maurice looked down on this bank holiday fun, feeling immensely superior. What would all those people think, if they knew he had walked on this beach – in real life – nearly two hundred years ago. He remembered the first dream: with the "packet" out at sea, and the smugglers talking about brandy and lace. He didn't even know, in those days, that a "packet" was the channel ferry, and a "beaver" was a hat. And freighters full of coal used to land where the Palace Pier was now. Thanks to the local history group he knew that everything he'd seen in the dream experiences, even things that he had thought were nonsense, were quite real.

He wasn't sure yet exactly how it happened. Vibrations, imprints from the past . . . perhaps it was something to do with the cemetery's magnetic field. "Anyway it's mine, whatever it is," muttered Maurice. "I may be a leprous repulsive little weed, but I'm a real time-traveller. Only the second in the world . . . ."

One of the skinhead photographers was looking at him oddly. The present day seafront, which had faded into a mist, became solid again. Maurice hurried back to see what had become of his great aunt. They took a taxi back. It was Maurice's idea. He insisted on paying for it, and Aunt Ada to his disappointment didn't protest at all. This increased his suspicion that she knew very well that she was being interrogated.

Buried in the tall hedge along the red drive there was a little wicket gate and beyond it a dark narrow path that led to the bottom section of the graveyard. Nobody came here. The weeds grew tall, and years of dead leaves silted up the paths. It was like an Aztec city half buried in jungle.

Maurice the archaeologist pored over inscriptions and scraped away moss to find dates, while over his head bees hummed and throbbed in a lost avenue of lime trees. He wasn't going to go to the magic carpet today. He thought he had reached a stage where he ought to sort out his ideas and think of a way to get more control over what happened. The carpet had a will of its own. He had tried thinking himself back to some famous event, like the Battle of Waterloo, but it just didn't work. He reminded himself to stop thinking about the "magic carpet". He ought to call it the "phenomenon location". Magic carpet sounded childish.

It was a warm day, and very warm down in the buried Aztec city. The bees hummed heavily. Maurice sat down with his back against a lime tree. He wasn't at all afraid of the pollen. He'd come to believe that nothing in here would hurt him. The birds were singing, the grass was full of flowers. Over his head floated clouds of gold green leaves. The solemn copper beeches that hid the funeral church were turning from bright ruby to deep purple. Peace, perfect peace, thought Maurice. It wasn't the most inspired sort of inscription, but he could see why it was so popular.

On the grave beside him someone had planted an old-fashioned white rose bush. It had tangled all over the mound and the flowers were opening now: white petals uncurling round golden polleny hearts. Maurice admired them unafraid. As the doctors always said, his asthma came from nerves more than from any outside source. Hundreds of years, millions of years had gone into producing those flowers. That was what great aunt's quotation meant:

. . . *Oh, no man knows*
Through what wild centuries, roves back the rose.

It was a subtle thought. He liked it. And all the people dead and resting here were part of that progress too. Flowing on and on, like a clear river . . . .

He didn't know how long he sat there before he started to feel uncomfortable. It was as if some unpleasant influence was competing with the perfect peace, and gradually getting the upper hand. Really, he knew, it was the hot sun that was getting to him – or else the steady, steady silence. When you are alone in a lonely place thoughts of being sneaked up upon are bound to arise, from time to time. It is Moth, he thought, and looked around. But there was no one behind him, only urns and pillars and the bees buzzing round the flowers. Then he saw, with a slightly guilty feeling of relief, that the black and white tom cat was sitting on a plinth a few urns away. It was often about. Moth teased it, but Maurice wouldn't have dared. It was a rough-looking customer.

"Oh, it's you," he said cheerfully. "Puss, puss –"

The tom cat took no notice. It was definitely nobody's pet. It laid its ears back and looked at something – the way cats do – slightly to Maurice's right and behind him, then it dropped into a sneaking crouch and hurried away. Maurice decided not to look and then he did look and naturally there was nothing. He got up, dusted bits of leaf from the seat of his trousers defiantly, and strolled casually but quickly to the gate.

It was a Saturday. He retired to his room and soon had books spread open all over his bed and propped up on the survival kit: he was very busy. He knew the front door was open, he could hear Mr Finch going in and out to get to the garden (he was painting great aunt's shed roof). So he wasn't completely surprised when he saw Moth standing in the door of his room. Except at her cheek.

"Hello, Maurice," she said. "I've come to see you."

"You've got a nerve, walking into people's houses. I suppose it was you in the cemetery wasn't it. Following me around again. I knew there was someone there."

Moth was looking at the medicines, poking and squeezing

things inquisitively. "Oh," she said. "Have they started playing their games? Well, I did warn you."

"Stupid girl," muttered Maurice, busily turning the pages of a big book of pictures. "I know it was you."

Moth knew about the magic carpet (or phenomenon location). But for some extraordinary reason she just wasn't interested. He was glad to see her really. It was a relief to be able to talk to someone who already knew the secret. Especially since she wasn't going to try and share the glory.

"Look," he told her, flicking the pages. "That's Chanctonbury Ring without the trees on it. I've seen it. I'm the only person in the world . . . ."

"No, you're not."

"What? Oh, you mean in the past. Yes, exactly. That's what makes this such a tremendous discovery –"

"You're only seeing what other people have seen."

Maurice stared at her. "Oh, I give up".

But he had to share his excitement, and Moth was the only audience available.

"You see, naturally the vibrations, the imprints, are strongest from the people buried there. But I've been looking at the oldest graves today. D'you realise if someone died in 1830 she could have been alive ninety years before that. She could have been in the French Revolution in 1793. Or even the American War of Independence! See this: there was a Stone Age settlement just near here. And there would have been Romans. Look at all the Roman villas people find. When I learn to control this thing better I could meet Julius Caesar . . . ."

"I don't think so," said Moth. "They wouldn't be well enough preserved."

"I'm not talking about digging up remains," protested Maurice. "This is far more exciting. You just don't listen."

Moth had lost interest. She was peering at his family photographs.

"Have you got a camera, Maurice?"

"Ummph."

He did have, but he wasn't going to say so. You can't be too careful with kids from problem families who walk into other people's houses without invitation. He looked up, because she'd gone quiet, and caught her posing hopefully in front of the window, with her hands coyly tucked under her chin.

"You look ridiculous. I wish you'd go away. I'm busy."

Moth stamped. "Come on," she said. "Come on into the garden. I want to show you something."

He had to follow her. She wasn't safe alone. When he got to the back door he looked first to the shed, his heart in his mouth. But Mr Finch was still peacefully painting, and his ladder was still in place.

"Moth, where are you?"

"Here. Catch!"

A ball of thin green twine came hurtling through the air: she was up in the laburnum tree that stooped over the outhouse beside the kitchen. He thought, indignantly, that he recognised the twine.

"Where did you get this?"

"From your aunt's gardening cupboard. See: there are hooks in the tree. Now that goes through there –"

Maurice had often puzzled, sitting over his breakfast or his tea, over a strange array of sturdy hooks painted the same faded pink as the breakfast room walls. Moth had found some more. Without asking permission, she cheerfully pulled up the breakfast room window and hopped inside. There were grooves in the frame, well worn and painted over, obviously meant to take the twine.

"What are you doing?"

She hopped out again. "The mirrors went here and here," she said. "And the camera here. Would your camera fit?"

"Of course it would." There was room for about twenty cameras in the crook of the laburnum.

"The professor's was a big one. I expect it was better than yours."

Suddenly Maurice realised what it was all about.

"Why, it's a trap!" he cried. "It's a fairy trap!"

Moth giggled and nodded, her eyes sparkling through the yellow laburnum flowers.

There sat the professor, lurking in his breakfast room. He watched his cunningly placed mirrors, using his control strings to adjust the view. Then when the fairy stepped into shot – a tug on the shutter and snap! It was captured for ever.

Maurice stopped laughing. He saw the joke. But if Professor Baxter was to be taken seriously as a scientist, this business about "ephemeral creatures" must be forgotten.

"Oh shut up. What do you know about it? It's probably something my great aunt rigged up to scare the birds."

Mr Finch peered suspiciously from the shed roof. The laburnum branches were shaking wildly but Moth had disappeared.

"Oh no –"

He hurried into the house, and caught her on the landing in front of Aunt Ada's room. Maurice nearly choked. His great aunt was inside, having her afternoon nap. He whispered and threatened from the top of the stairs like someone trying to recapture an escaped monkey.

She was off again. She vanished into the Professor's bedroom, and the room that had been his upstairs dining room. There was nothing to be seen, only a double bed with no covers on it, and some anonymous furniture. Maurice had established this ages ago. He took a quick look round: nothing was disturbed – came out on the landing to see a pair of bare brown feet kicking above his head. She had climbed on the banister rail, and was disappearing into the loft.

"Moth!"

She was gone. There was nothing for it, Maurice had to climb too, using the shelves of a cupboard by the Professor's bedroom door as steps up to the trap door. His head came up into dusky space. There was a wasp's nest, round and grey like a transplanted brain, clinging to a beam in a corner.

"Come on, Maurice."

This was definitely breaking and entering, but what could he do? He couldn't phone the police. He didn't want to be the person who got her put in care. He clambered out, horribly afraid of what the fibreglass insulation would do to his lungs.

"Now, Moth, don't be silly –"

She was crouched over a pile of debris, that the insulation layers had heaped up against the chimney breast on the downhill wall. Maurice fell over a clump of hard squashy little sacks, and nearly put his foot through the floor between two joists. Part of the debris was a cardboard box. It was empty, except for three or four small books, furry with dust . . . .

Maurice forgot all about Moth. He picked one out, and peered. He couldn't read the title. When he opened it, he found it was full of foreign poetry: he thought it was Latin.

"She didn't burn these. She forgot about them," murmured Moth.

Maurice opened another book. He was stunned to see crabby old handwriting. It was a diary.

They went back to Maurice's room. He took all the books. Only one of them was a diary. The others, when dusted off, turned out to be all Latin poetry: English on one side, Latin on the other. There were notes in the margins, he noticed. He put them aside: it was possible there might be something there in code. The diary entries stopped in the middle of the year. It was 1945, the year Professor Baxter died. Maurice was disappointed. The old scientist had burned his papers by that time. The great discovery must have come long before.

"You ought to read it," said Moth. "It would do you good."

She pattered off and started to play with his coloured map pins, sticking them round the edge of the Mediterranean.

Maurice looked up. His eyes narrowed. He had just realised that Moth had not been playing the fool after all, with her breaking and entering and peeking into empty bedrooms. She knew all about this house. Even about the "fairy trap". She'd been in here before, taking advantage of a vague old lady. Looking for what?

The answer was obvious. Her pretence of not being interested in time-travel was just a blind.

"You used to come here when you were a little boy, didn't you, Maurice?"

He looked at her coldly.

"Once or twice."

"I wasn't interested in you then. You were too young. You weren't allowed to go into the garden by yourself."

Maurice sneered. "I suppose you were just the same age as you are now."

"Of course I was."

She giggled maddeningly.

"I've had enough," said Maurice. "I know what your game is. You want the professor's secret. Just clear off. This is my great aunt's house and everything in it was left to her. So whatever I find is my family property. You'd better be careful or you're going to get into real trouble."

"I don't want anything," she smiled. "It's you who ought to be careful, Maurice."

"Clear off."

When she was gone, he remembered that the underside of the loft trap door was painted white and would be covered in telltale smudges. He had to clean it with a scouring pad and hot water, standing awkwardly up on the banister rail in his socks, so that Mary wouldn't ask questions.

Outside the kitchen door late afternoon sun poured over the laburnum tree so it was hard to tell what was light and what was flowers. Moth stood in the yellow shade looking up at Maurice's window, then she went over the wall, into that other garden. Mr Finch did not see her go.

Five

Maurice was marching. His feet felt awful, truly awful. The boots he was wearing didn't fit and he seemed to have put them on without any socks. If he'd dared he would have stepped out of line, but someone would have noticed and he didn't want to behave suspiciously. Besides, he couldn't. The dream experience was too real. He must march, with all these other marching bodies, with thick yellow clods of mud glueing themselves to his boots. All around them stretched a world so empty it looked as if a nuclear bomb had been dropped, if not several nuclear bombs. There were no bushes, no roads, no buildings, no grass, only a few starved looking skeletons of trees. The sky was grey and full of rolling clouds. He wanted to escape but he knew that time-traveller or not he didn't dare set off alone into that horrific emptiness. There were loops of barbed wire in places with tattered scraps that looked like old clothes flapping on them. Maurice winced, tried not to think of what they were.

Suddenly, part of the endless ploughed field jumped up in the air beside him. Someone yelled. He felt himself grabbed, shoved face down into the mud. His tin hat gouged into his forehead . . . . He was in a dark place. He thought it was a room, but when he looked down he saw mud oozing between the boards on the floor. There was a horrible smell. He tried to move and found it very difficult. Something had happened to one of his legs. When he tried to look at it all he could see was the oozing floorboards. A shadow moved. He hoped it was his foot but it wasn't. It was a big dirty rat . . . .

Maurice woke up and lay with open eyes. The blue sky overhead seemed dark, with fiery lights in it. He sat up and rubbed his eyes. The green hollow returned.

He knew where he had just been. He had seen similar scenes often enough, in films or on television. That was the First World War. Somewhere in France or maybe Belgium about seventy years ago. It would be interesting if he could work out exactly where and when. He might find out something they'd got wrong in all the history books. So Maurice told himself. But he was not convinced. He wondered if the battlefield at Agincourt had been such an unpleasant place. Probably – though of course it would have been smaller. Being a scientific time-traveller certainly wasn't all fun and games. They ought not to put that sort of thing on television, he thought indignantly. They wouldn't if they really knew.

He walked back by his usual route, but he was uneasy. He had a dismally familiar sensation: he stopped, near the bottom of the Columbarium steps, and peeled up his jeans. Sure enough, there was a red speckly rash. Perhaps he had been lying on a nettle. He peeled up the other leg and there it was, just the same. Symmetrical. No getting away from it, that's an allergy rash, said Maurice in a resigned voice, out loud. He turned around quickly. But whoever it was who had been watching, listening, was gone. Only the rose bushes with their neat black labels . . . .

"Who are you?" he shouted. "What do you want?"

No reply.

Maurice went home. Great aunt was invisible as usual, and Mary had already left. There was a colander of purple sprouting broccoli on the kitchen table. It looked utterly poisonous, a completely un-foodlike colour: like something the witch cons the trusting princess into eating in a Walt Disney fairytale. There was a note about beefburgers. He took a pack out of the freezer and read the label out of habit. They were the wrong kind. He could only eat the kind that had nothing but meat in them. He read the label five times more and then threw the frozen pack across the kitchen.

Stupid woman!

If I was poor, really poor, he thought. Like they used to be in Victorian days. I'd have died of allergies by now and it would be all over. Some of his recent time-travel experiences had made him think about things like that. In the end he picked up the beefburgers and put them back. He tipped the broccoli into the pedal bin, and took out his cake of gluten free bread from Aunt Ada's bread bin, where it lived in a special quarantined plastic box. He found some honey to go with it. No butter of course, and he hated gooey margarine.

But he must have done something wrong after all, because in spite of the antihistamine he took he woke up in the night with his mouth and throat swollen on the inside so he could hardly breathe. He had to crawl to the phone with the doctor's emergency number. Uncle Tom came rushing across town in case he had to be taken into hospital; then Auntie Sue took the morning off work to be with him.

"Them damn hamburgers," groaned Mary.

"I didn't eat them," said Maurice, unswollen again by the miracle of modern medicine.

"You touch them. I know that because they all bent. You drop them pretty hard, huh? Who can blame you? Maurice, we going to have to keep you in plastic bag, this rate of going."

The doctor said Maurice must never, never, never treat himself, even with things he'd been given before, and she took away half the survival kit. Maurice had been amassing it for years, and he knew a lot of it was no longer official. But the marching array of bottles and packets had given him a sort of satisfaction. He felt naked without it.

Mary offered to sleep in over the weekend, but Maurice was against the idea so it was given up. Anyway, the frightening throat swelling didn't come back, and the nettle rash just developed in its routine way, over his arms and legs mostly. Because of the season the doctor thought Maurice might be getting sensitive to pollens after all and ordered him indoors. Maurice didn't argue.

He couldn't sleep. His new prescription didn't do anything for the itching. He was reduced to useless creams and calamine lotion. He lay propped on his pillows listening to the quiet house. Tick, tick, tick. The stairs creaked. Great aunt had been long in bed, maybe it was a mouse, or just the old wood complaining. In his bedroom at Keymer Drive there was a street lamp outside the window and the curtains were light-weight. It was never really dark. He used to lie listening there, wheezing, thinking it was three in the morning and then the cars would start driving up. Lights on the ceiling, bang, slam: voices, footsteps – everybody coming home from the cinema or the pub. And he would know it was only eleven thirty, and there were hours and hours still to bear.

It was different here. The street was on the other side of the house and his curtains were thick. Night was black. He could only hear the faint murmur of traffic on the main road at the bottom of the hill, and even that seemed to have stopped now. The quiet darkness had seemed very restful when he first started sleeping here, but now, somehow, it had become unwelcome. He could switch on a light and read, but he didn't want to. It might attract Aunt Ada, the way a light attracted parents however asleep you thought they were. It might attract –

Don't be silly.

He would have liked to know the time, but his watch was on the cupboard under the map. His alarm clock must have been misplaced when the survival kit was attacked, he couldn't see any green numbers floating in the dark. If he groped around searching for it, the itching was bound to start up again. So he lay still.

He had seen Aunt Ada going into the cemetery two or three times now, carrying flowers. It was mysterious, because he knew all her family, her mother and father and so on, couldn't be buried there. They had lived somewhere completely different, the other side of Brighton. What made it even more interesting was her arthritis. If it was so hard for her to get about, she surely wouldn't bother except for something very important. But he had never caught her anywhere near the Columbarium.

Professor Baxter came to live in the house in Brighton about 1930. He went on with his secret research for another ten years, before he went dotty and burned it all. All that time, Aunt Ada kept house for him. She must know something. Something must have made it worth her while to stay with the Professor. She must have been quite young then, in order to be still alive now. Why didn't she get married, at least, instead of wasting her life on a doddery old man.

After he gave up his work he started going really dotty. At the end of the war his married daughter took him to live in Oxford again, but he died quite soon. He left Great Aunt Ada the house, and some money. His family was annoyed. They claimed he wasn't responsible. They got a doctor to give evidence that he had been suffering from persecution mania before he died. But the lawyers said the will had been made a good few years before, so that didn't matter.

Maurice had been able to refresh his memory about the old story by talking to Auntie Sue. But even then, she didn't seem to like the subject. Kept telling him it was none of his business to root around in Aunt Ada's past.

Nothing happened to the Professor, anyway, he thought. He died in his bed.

Perhaps that was an unfortunate phrase to use, just at the moment. He meant, of course, the Professor never ended up stuck in one of the unpleasant parts of the past. Nothing more .... He sat up, elbowing darkness aside as if it was something solid, got out of bed and padded to the window. When he opened the thick curtains and pushed aside the lace, dark vanished. The sky was bright blue, deep and intense. The moon must be somewhere, right above the house maybe, and the stars were twinkling brightly. In Aunt Ada's garden he could see everything but colour, even the separate flowers.

He was thinking of his parents. His healthy boring parents. What was so wonderful about having a mother who sold boats. She'd only been doing it part time anyway, since Tabitha was born. He didn't even know what his father did, precisely, but it wasn't very interesting. They were just very ordinary people and they had gone away and abandoned Maurice because he was a sickly nuisance. A leprous wimp, despised by Jasmin Kapoor, sneered at by everyone. Better face it. The only good thing in his life was the magic carpet he had found in King Death's Garden. He deserved it, to make up for everything. And he wasn't going to give it up.

Over the wall the headstones stood etched in black on the stiff grey grass, with their shadows lying before them clear as inkblots. He could see the bench – Colonel someone or other – standing on the path near the wall.

That's funny –

He thought he saw something move but when he looked again it was only a dark little shrub standing near the Colonel, as if it was leaning on him. The moonlight was playing tricks. If he stared any longer he could easily believe some of those inkblot shadows, especially near aunt's wall, were lying on the wrong side of the stones . . . .

Rubbish!

He let the curtain drop and went back to bed.

Maurice was off school for a week. It was just his luck the week happened to be half term. The itching weals on his arms and legs gradually subsided into a pattern of red circles, as if he had been fighting with an octopus. On either Monday or Tuesday morning, Mr Finch came in and complained to Mary about the garden. Someone had been throwing things over the wall.

He was always complaining about next door down the hill, sneakily exporting their snails after dark, but this was different. Dead leaves, said Mr Finch. It's very unsightly. Lord knows where they come from, at this time of year. He suspected Maurice had something to do with it. He was a retired policeman and had a natural instinct about boys.

But although Aunt Ada talked as if Mr Finch was her private gardener he was only a handyman, coming in for a few hours a week. He didn't matter. Besides, Maurice had decided he must have been lightheaded from antihistamines the night he looked out of the window and started frightening himself.

"How come you never itch that rash?" Mary demanded. 'You have to tie my hands in bags to keep my fingers off that right now, never mind how young you are.''

"Habit," said Maurice boredly. "If you scratch them they go into blisters and it just gets nastier. You roll on them in the night and they break and there's raw flesh –''

"Maurice, be quiet! You make my skin scream.''

He had meant to. It was Wednesday and he was in the kitchen with her because he had to eat, and he was sick of lurking in his room. But he wished she'd leave him alone. Mary studied him thoughtfully.

"You got something on your mind.''

"Yes. A rotten rash.''

"But where did it come from, Maurice? You never ate anything wrong. What else you been up to?''

"I'm going back upstairs," said Maurice coldly. "If you're going to use the vacuum cleaner, at least don't sing. I'm supposed to rest.''

He got up to go. The outhouse door was open to let in the sunny afternoon. A little heap of damp dark leaves had drifted in again, huddling up the kitchen doorstep as if they were trying to sneak into the house.

"Now where did that come from?" muttered Mary. "I swear I just swept that floor.''

Maurice glanced at the leaves, and hurried away to his room.

But still, the moment his rash was half-healed, he went back to King Death's Garden.

It was hot. Unbelievably hot, so that sweat broke out all over Maurice's skin, and trickled with frantically irritating effect over the remains of his rash. He was wearing, he noticed, whitish coloured trousers like ski pants. Very fashionable, but far too clinging for this climate. But he didn't mind the heat because the place was so exciting. He'd only ever been abroad once, and quietly hated it (Spain) so his parents never tried it again. He decided he would have to change his mind. Except, of course, for the Do'an. He walked through a market place where they were selling dried fish with spines down their backs, and sharks' fins; and exciting dark oriental things piled in front of little smoky doorways. He wanted to sketch and sketch . . . .

Four little men went by, carrying a box on poles. The tassled curtain lifted and a Chinese girl looked out of the box, in a brocade dress with her hair piled up and skewered with pins. She had a lot of makeup on her eyes; she smiled at Maurice.

He sat under a palm tree, with fronded leaves silver in the sunlight, and looked out over the red stone town to the blue, blue sea. So hot! He was drawing, with sweat running down his fingers, when he saw on a rock right next to him a lizard about two feet long (including tail) coloured bright pink and blue. Carefully he put down his brush and grabbed –

– and found himself back in the garden with his hand cupped against cool grass. For a moment he could still feel, in his palms and fingers, the tingling from where they'd hit harsh, hot rock.

It was very weird. He had tried to bring things back before. He knew that it might be unwise to move anything important, but he thought just a leaf or a stone couldn't do much damage to the space-time continuum. It never worked. One minute the thing was there in his hand. The next moment it just melted away, as he woke up. He had decided this must be one of the unbreakable laws of time travel.

He was relieved to have had a good dream for a change. They had all been good at first, but now some of them were turning nasty. He didn't want to visit the trenches again. That rat! Although, of course, it wasn't real. Not for Maurice, anyway.

That place had been so like an exotic travel poster he wasn't even sure it was in the past. Of course it probably was: but quite obviously not the past of anyone who lived in Brighton a hundred years ago. So his theory was confirmed. The vibrations could be from anywhere in time. They weren't *particularly* connected with this cemetery. He looked round the hollow, at the quiet leaning stones and the blurred angel. Not that it would make any difference to a scientific observer, where the vibrations or imprints actually came from. However, it was better to get these things sorted out. Especially if the observer had started getting silly unscientific ideas . . . .

He passed the Columbarium, and ahead of him was the quiet lawn, dappled with leaf shadows from the trees that stood about here and there on the grass. Maurice came to a halt. There seemed to be someone sitting on the bench that belonged to Felicia May Dalton, Beloved Wife and Mother.

He stepped behind a tree and looked out. He was not sure about the figure. It could be just a passerby who had stepped in through the Fairsea gate for a moment's rest. The outline was rather indistinct, it might be just a shadow . . . Maurice felt annoyed. Two can play at that game, he thought. He turned and quickly, silently, returned to the hollow. The wallflowers were over, but the pink valerian had grown up bushy and tall, filling the air with its musty scent. Maurice noticed that it was attracting a lot of butterflies: tortoiseshells mostly, with their wings a little grey and tattered as if they had just come out of hibernation.

He didn't spare them much of a glance. Grinning to himself,

he dived into a small footpath half buried in bramble. Luckily he had thoroughly explored this territory, before the magic carpet took over his life completely. A few minutes later, after some scuffles with the bramble thickets, he emerged safe and sound down in the Aztec city where the lime trees grew.

But the game continued. He thought he was all right because the main drive was on the other side of the hedge, with cars liable to pass and gardeners at work. Then he looked back down an avenue of lost tombs, and distinctly saw something dark hopping quickly out of sight behind an obelisk.

He left the Aztec city briskly. On the drive he felt safe, until he passed a certain memorial that had always fascinated him. It belonged to a family called Clairmont, and took the form of a huge bronze door. It had pillars on either side, big elaborate hinges and even a lock with a keyhole. It looked so self-important, this door, that Maurice had often been tempted to knock on it (there was a bronze knocker) and run away. He didn't feel like doing that now. But the moment he passed it, he knew it was opening behind him. He whipped around. Nothing –

At the end of the drive the main gates to the cemetery stood in plain sight. There were cars passing on the road, there was the back of the notice telling dogs to stay out: No Dogs Allowed Except on Legitimate Business. As if dogs could read. He would not be scared into making a bolt for it. If he let that happen, he'd never be able to come in here again. Besides, to get to those gates now he would have to walk right by the bronze door.

Round the funeral church, up the shrubbery steps. It's only Moth playing silly games . . . . He had not seen her since he chucked her out of his room. Which was fair enough, really. As he passed the spot where they had hidden and watched the bluetits, he noticed something lying on the ground between the roots of the sycamore tree: a draggled trail of dead grass and bits of wool with sad little shapes in it. That rotten tomcat, he thought, imagining the cruel claws groping inwards.

He was through the gap in the wall, breathing a sigh of

unscientific relief, when he saw someone sitting on a bench. There was no doubt about it this time. A tall old man in a tweed jacket. It looked very like the old man he had seen in here once before . . . .

Maurice had been playing the fool. He didn't really believe he was being chased. He was ashamed of his own imaginary fears: and he'd decided to make a game of them. That was all. Or nearly all. But that solid tweed-clad figure was something different. He couldn't say why. He didn't wait to see if the old man disappeared as before – his nerve just snapped and he ducked for cover, hopping from headstone to headstone over the graves, straight for the gates.

Died suddenly at Dagenham . . . The Time was short, the Shock severe . . . Was taken into Heavenly Rest . . . On the Fourteenth of September 1940, as a result of enemy action . . .

He wasn't used to such exertion. He was already breathless when he staggered out onto the home stretch of the path – straight into a painful collision with a large substantial body, and a bicycle.

He could see, as soon as he picked himself up, that she had been watching everything.

"What you sneaking about the graves for like that?" demanded Mary. "You playing hide-and-seek? That's not very reverent, Maurice. I would have thought you know better than that behaviour."

She peered around narrowly. "Where's your friends gone? They all run off and left you?"

Maurice shrugged. He tried to get by, but she had hold of his arm. She looked into his face, long and thoughtfully.

"You look scared, Maurice."

"I've just been run over."

Mary took no notice of that. She went on holding his arm and looking at him in silence.

"Maurice," she said at last. "You know, you never get a fair deal, *never* off of the black market. I tell you because I know."

"I'm sure you're a world authority," said Maurice. "That's why they call it the black market, I suppose. Leave me alone."

He twisted his arm free and marched away. She didn't follow him. He noticed, as he walked by, that there was no tree or shrub growing anywhere near the Colonel's bench.

That night Maurice wrote to his parents. Aunt Ada was asleep, the house was quiet. He lay on his bed with the thin airmail paper resting on his maths folder. *The girl at school, Jasmin, that I told you about, isn't really a major friend. I just liked her for a while. Actually I'm not going to send you my science project to look at after all. It wasn't a school thing. It was just my own idea. I'm thinking of giving it up anyway . . . . I don't want long-sleeved teeshirts. I think they look stupid, I'll wear shirts, or use a lot of sunscreen.*

He wrote for a while with his back to the door, then turned round so he was facing it. Then he got up and opened the door and looked out. A few minutes later he got up again and went out on to the landing. He switched on the stairs light and left it on, and went back to his letter . . . *Anyway it's very good weather here and I hope it is the same with you . . . .*

Six

The laburnum's flowers became litter on the outhouse roof, and Mary swept them off with a broom. Aunt Ada's old-fashioned roses opened their heavy petals, and the sweet peas tenderly raised by Mr Finch fluttered like butterflies on their trellis. In the upper cemetery long grass swept almost to the tops of the headstones, and the smaller paths were drowned in white frothy cow parsley. Further down in the depths of the Garden, green piled on green, muffling everything in a rich warm silence that seemed to listen to every footstep.

Maurice never looked forward to the summer. It was a bad time of year for allergies. Not only was he allergic to strong sunlight itself, but a single insect bite could swell up violently and send him to bed. He went about with his sleeves buttoned down and his collar buttoned up to his chin, and his face plastered with sunscreen. He hated going to the sea because he was always so white and usually covered in some ghastly leprosy – should he dare to undress. He couldn't eat any of the famous summer things. Strawberries and cream produced weals in half an hour. And when he refused the adults said "Poor Maurice", but he knew they were secretly annoyed. Even his own parents, who should know better.

This summer was no improvement. All the pleasure that he'd found in the garden with Moth seemed to be over. Without explaining to himself why, he was beginning to feel a sneaking relief about the flight to the Do'an, looming up at the end of term. There would be nothing green and shadowy about a skyscraper flat in Ishar. But at the same time, he couldn't imagine how he was going to tear himself away from King Death's Garden.

He had an unpleasant experience one day in Fairsea library. It was lunchtime. Mrs Wray was talking to Carole Verne at the counter, about developments in the local history project. Maurice was changing Great Aunt's books for her (she liked westerns: Louis L'Amour, Zane Grey). He was looking in the oversized picture book section, just killing time because he didn't want to talk to Carole. He came across a thin volume of old travel pictures. They were prints of watercolours of the Far East, done by a naval officer. Maurice leaved through the pages, not sure why he was interested in this particular book. He saw palm trees with silvery fronds, and Chinese looking people trotting around. Four little men with pigtails carrying a tassled box. The box looked far too small to be comfortable for the girl who was looking out from under the curtain. This last picture was a street scene in Malacca, a port in Malaya, circa 1810. It was quite a good drawing, and uneasily familiar.

Maurice suddenly had no doubt that he was looking at the place and time of his "exotic travel poster" dream. He turned to the front of the book and found that the artist was born and died in Brighton . . . .

As he read, somebody came up and stood close behind him, breathing down his neck. He caught a strong whiff of musty bad breath. He looked round, annoyed, expecting to find one of the decrepit old unemployed blokes who haunted the library. There was no one there.

He had a good look at the Latin poetry books that used to belong to Professor Baxter. They were volumes of Vergil's *Aeneid*. He found no clues, just the kind of underlining and notes in the margins that someone might make if they were having to learn the stuff at school. The "poetry" was pretty turgid even in English, making Maurice glad no one had ever forced him to learn Latin. The only thing he learned now was that Professor Baxter had been morbidly keen on Book Six, where Aeneas the hero goes down into the underworld and meets a lot of dead people. That part was full of underlinings.

Aeneas's adventures in the underworld had a bad effect on Maurice's nerves. Almost every night he would wake up in the dark, sure he could hear someone moving about downstairs. It was the Professor, of course, come to reclaim his property. Once he opened his eyes (dreaming) and the tweedy old gentleman he had twice seen in the graveyard was standing right beside his bed. A voice in his ear whispered distinctly: *innumerable as the leaves, their hands reach out in longing for the farther shore* . . . Maurice woke up terrified and had to have the light on for the rest of the night. But even so he could still see them, just as they were described in the Aeneas story. The crowds of thin ghastly figures with their mouths open and faces like leather; groping and grasping on the side of a dark river. He was disgusted to think that people used to teach that sort of story in school. And then they had the cheek to complain about video nasties!

Mary kept muttering about the dead leaves that drifted into her kitchen, sneaking under the outhouse door. Maurice avoided her like the plague. But she'd become rather sulky and silent with him anyway – staring at him with a broody expression at times, and shaking her head.

One day he came up the shrubbery steps and nearly bolted when he saw someone sitting on a bench at the end of the path. But it was only Mr Kidder the gardener eating his tea out of a plastic box. He beckoned Maurice to come over and join him, and offered him a bread and jam sandwich.

"No, thank you. I can't eat ordinary bread."

The old gardener sighed contentedly, surveying his domain. "Lovely day isn't it," he remarked. "And a lovely place, and we've got it all to ourselves, as per usual. People in this world walk around with buckets over their heads, in my opinion. It's all shops and cars and motorways and never time to sit and appreciate something green."

Maurice sat and looked, over the graves and the treetops of the valley; and beyond to the hazy downs and the blue sky. He remembered the distant age when he used to walk through here in the spring, squeezing a bit of comfort out of the trees and flowers. He used to think then that the cemetery was such a peaceful place. He shivered.

"You're not cold are you?" exclaimed Mr Kidder. "You've got thin blood if you're cold on a day like this!"

Maurice did not care for that expression. Sometimes now after he'd been on the magic carpet he did feel "thinned", as if he was living more and more in the experiences and there was less of him to come back to the present. But there's no choice now, he thought. I just have to keep going back.

Mr Kidder was complaining about the young louts the Council supplied for him. They could never be found when they were wanted, but they were always sneaking around, annoying him. They hid behind hedges and muttered . . . he was going to catch them at it one of these days. Maurice smiled uneasily. He could have sympathised with Mr Kidder about that problem. Or he might have asked him about another irritation. That tall elderly gentleman in old-fashioned clothes who stood and stared, and then vanished. But he decided against it.

"Have you seen my friend recently?" he asked instead. The wild flowery grass made him think of Moth. He imagined her hiding in it, spying on the fieldmice.

"Your friend?"

"You know. The girl with dark hair. You've seen me with her I suppose – er, messing about."

He finished uncertainly, remembering who was the favourite victim of Moth's "messing". But Mr Kidder looked puzzled rather than annoyed.

"Dark curly hair," suggested Maurice. "She wears funny clothes – sometimes she takes her shoes off. I think she comes from that street by the racecourse."

Mr Kidder scowled. "That lot never comes in here," he declared. "Not likely, not while I'm around. Bar the lads after conkers in the autumn, I don't know that I've seen any kids in here, on their own account, except you. I've seen you playing some funny games all right, but always by yourself."

Maurice stared. "But I know you've seen her. She practically lives here!"

Mr Kidder shook his head. "Now don't you try making a monkey out of me –"

He was being ridiculous. No doubt he didn't like Moth, but really it was absurd to pretend she didn't exist.

Maurice went home and found his great aunt in her parlour arranging sweet peas in a silver rose bowl. She was more perky now. The heat had caused her arthritis to retreat. For an eighty-year-old she looked quite hale and hearty – especially when compared with Maurice. She had opened the heavy curtains, and sunshine poured in over the old piano with its candle holders, the plush covered furniture and the monster roses on the walls. She had her sweet peas spread out on the little round table on a piece of newspaper. She was singing to herself as she arranged them, something about "fairy gifts fading away . . . ."

"Aunt Ada," said Maurice. "Do you know anything about a girl who lives round here? I think she must know you. She knows all about Professor Baxter. I've just realised I haven't seen her for ages . . . ."

She smiled at him vaguely. "They are creatures of the moment" she explained gently. "You can't keep them long." She must be talking about the sweet peas.

He went slowly upstairs and sat on his bed. Was it possible his imagination had been playing tricks on him? Was Moth just a friend he'd made up for himself? He was feeling slightly odd these days, from sleeping so badly. It almost seemed as if it could be true that Moth had never been real. Just a breeze in the long grass: bright bold eyes made of sunlight winking between leaves ... Maurice pulled himself together. It was hardly likely he would have made her up for company when he didn't actually like her much.

He got up and looked out into his great aunt's garden. And there was Moth, by the rosebushes. She must have climbed over the wall, she couldn't have come through the house this time. Trespassing again! She was wearing a pink and pale blue dress with a short frilly skirt, looking quite well cared for and fashionable for a change. Trust her to go climbing walls in an outfit like that. She looked up: he saw her grinning cheekily.

"Moth! Leave that trellis alone!"

He pelted down the stairs, but when he got to the lawn she was gone. He stood in a cloud of scent from the sweet peas, frowning in confusion.

It was a relief to get to school these days, to the real world of smelly corridors and reading bits of *Kes* round the class. By now he was the only person at Fairsea, the only white person anyway, who hadn't picked up the slightest trace of a suntan. The ordinary boy had a bright red face and moaned when his shoulders were gently touched. He peeled bits of his arms off in class, making his neighbours retch and gag. This gave Maurice some satisfaction. And at least, he thought, nothing mysterious or shadowy could survive the company of 2M, or any staff or pupils of Fairsea Comprehensive. He was safe from the silly things that he kept imagining.

But he was wrong.

The local history group was still active. Carole Verne's father was putting together a new exhibition: "Brighton in the Thirties". On Wednesdays when the library shut at four Mrs Wray the librarian stayed on for an hour. Instead of hiding in a corner, the enthusiasts spread themselves, unfolding the display screens and scattering photographs all over the floor.

Maurice had lost interest in the group before half term. But one Wednesday at the end of June he went with Carole and

Andrew to the library. He wanted his time-travel drawings back.

He discovered that he'd become a celebrity. Mr Verne (– call me Alec) had shown no interest in the pictures when Maurice first produced them. Obviously he considered Maurice disabled, because of the asthma fit he had witnessed – and therefore incapable of producing anything interesting. But now he'd studied them, and he was amazed. He took it for granted Maurice had copied the sketches out of books. But they were very clever anyway.

"Where did you find this early nineteenth century view of the Thames, Maurice? Such a lot of detail –"

"I don't know. I suppose I just imagined what it would have been like."

Carole Verne leaned over Maurice's shoulder, breathing down his neck. "I like this one of the Chain Pier in the storm. It looks really real . . . ."

In another world, he would have been delighted. It wasn't often Maurice Eastman managed to shine. And Jasmin Kapoor, his ex-idol, was sitting at the next table. She was fitting the old Regent Cinema into her model of North St in the Thirties, but he knew she was listening. But now he just wished Mr Verne would change the subject. It made him uncomfortable.

"Excuse me Mr Verne – er, Alec. There's someone at the door."

He got up to open it, glad of the excuse to escape. The library forecourt was empty.

"It was probably the cleaners, Maurice. But they can't chuck us out yet."

Maurice sorted old photographs with an off-duty staff nurse. Jasmin Kapoor left her model, and came over with one of his drawings.

"I didn't know you could draw so well," she said. "But see here – this perspective is wrong. Would you like me to show you?"

Maurice looked up at his ex-idol, trying to decide whether she was being really friendly or just pretending. He didn't hate her anymore for those insults she had showered on him. After all, he had caught her with her boyfriend. Nobody likes being spied on.

Behind Jasmin's back, the library door opened again all by itself.

"All right, ignore me," said Jasmin, and walked off back to the model table, her shoulders sharp with annoyance.

Mrs Wray went across and turned the key in the lock, muttering something about subsidence.

The history group was oddly subdued that afternoon. A couple of people decided not to stay: the staff nurse remembered an urgent appointment. Twice Mrs Wray went out to see why the school cleaners were hanging about in the forecourt. A third time she was gone for several mintues and came back frowning.

"There seems to be an animal loose on the site. Does it belong to anyone here?"

"What sort of an animal?" asked Jasmin.

"A dog, I suppose. A big dog."

No one knew anything about a big dog.

"Let's break up early," said Mr Verne. "It's getting so dark, I think we're in for a downpour."

But it must have been just a cloud passing over – as Carole said. Outside the June sun was still shining brightly in a clear blue sky.

Mrs Wray wanted to put some of Maurice's pictures on display, though they weren't connected with the Thirties. She pursued him down the drive with this offer, making him jump wildly as a hand landed on his shoulder. He declined the honour and hurried away, clutching his folder of drawings as if he was trying to hide them.

In his room, late at night, Maurice read the Professor's diary. He wouldn't have chosen to start reading it after dark. But in her perked up state Aunt Ada had become unusually active. She had looked in twice during the evening, once to invite him down for tea and biscuits, once to bring him a cooling drink of lemon and barley water. Even she seemed to have noticed something was wrong. He hoped she wouldn't write to his parents about it. He knew she did write. He had seen her wavery spider handwriting on the airmail forms she left on the hall stand, for Mary to take down to the post. It was past eleven before he could be sure of reading without interruption.

He no longer thought the year 1945 was uninteresting. He wasn't looking for a secret formula. He wanted to find out exactly what was happening to Professor Baxter, when everybody thought he was going really mad – in the last months before he died.

The old Professor's handwriting was as hard to read as Aunt Ada's. But it was easy to see why people had thought he was dotty. There were all sorts of references; half told stories – that Maurice could only understand because he knew about travelling in time. He noticed the professor seemed to have gone a lot further back. But "the method" didn't really work for "the remote periods". What was recovered was too fragmentary, too corrupted. He had had much better results from more recent material. There was a list, at one point, of names and dates. It looked rather as if it had been copied from the stone records in King Death's Garden. The hair on the back of Maurice's neck prickled as he read it.

Occasionally he lifted his head and listened. There seemed to be a sort of busy silence outside his door, as if several very soft-footed people were walking up and down the stairs and pacing in front of his room. But he could hear nothing.

Still sleeping badly. NB remind Miss Drew to buy nerve food.

Maurice noticed his door was slightly ajar. It was a few minutes before he could make up his mind to get up and shut it. There was definitely some whispering going on outside. "I don't know what you're on about. I don't know what you want from me," he muttered. Suddenly he flung the door open, flicked on the light switch and shouted.

"Go away!"

The shadows on the landing did not scatter. They moved, as if they were turning their faces towards him. Maurice slammed the door and stood with his back to it, breathing fast.

"Maurice? Is that you?"

He looked out again, very cautiously. The landing was bright and empty, and Aunt Ada was standing at her door in a dressing gown, peering without her glasses.

"I thought I heard you cry out."

"Yes – er, I shut the door on my finger. Sorry . . . ."

He put the book away under his pillow. Then he changed his mind and put it in the bottom drawer of the wardrobe. It was a while before he could make himself switch off the light. "Vibrations," whispered Maurice defiantly. "Vibrations, and harmless chemical patterns."

Seven

For the first time, he managed to stay away from King Death's Garden altogether. He knew he was being unscientific, but the side effects were getting to be beyond a joke. He had to try and work out what could be done to get the bugs out of Professor Baxter's discovery, before he used it again. He needed time.

No time was allowed.

For three nights the busy silence outside his room was still, and he slept in peace. On the fourth day, 2M had a double lesson of computer studies at the end of the afternoon, with Mr Stewart in the computer room. The computer room was in the 1960 building, next to the science labs. There were six micros. The rest of the class drew flowcharts, tried to write programs and answered the questions on the end of last week's worksheet, if they hadn't done so already. Mr Stewart, who preferred to teach physics, was feeling harassed as usual. He did not notice that Maurice Eastman was behaving oddly: not unlike a nervous shoplifter, or a person expecting to be kneecapped by the Mafia.

Maurice sat where he could watch the classroom door. He ought to feel safe but he didn't. Every so often he gave a little start and looked over his shoulder quickly. It could have been to make sure Mr Stewart wasn't approaching. There was not much going on in Maurice's computer notebook.

About half way through the lesson, when the first bell had just gone, he had a turn on one of the machines.

"Come on, Maurice. Where's that nice little program you wrote for me? Save the doodling and daydreaming for when you haven't done any work."

Mr Stewart was talking about second year physics.

Maurice typed in the first lines of his program. He still kept looking round. Ever since this lesson started, he had been hearing someone whisper "Maurice –" right in his ear. The whisper was very distinct, even through the normal classroom noise. He hoped someone was playing a joke.

On another bench, Carole Verne, Jason Trevor and Andrew Bolt were hovering round a machine. Andrew had loaded a game cassette. They were taking turns to play, with the sound turned off, giggling and concealing the screen from Mr Stewart.

"Is that it?" said a voice over his shoulder.

It was the ordinary boy: otherwise known as David Bollom. Maurice looked at his screen and saw that the three lines of program had disappeared. Instead there was Maurice's name, rising in an endless column up the middle.

"I did that ages ago," remarked the ordinary boy scornfully. "That's kidstuff."

maurice, said the screen. maurice MAURICE MAURICE ... The seven letters grew enormous. They shrank, and turned into a spiral, spinning outwards with every arm saying mauricemauricemaurice . . . .

"Cor! Hey, Stewpot! Come and look what we've done!"

Maurice whimpered faintly. He hit the escape button. He hit Break and CLS. No effect . . . .

"What's going on?" said Mr Stewart.

The screen was blank.

He was forced to start typing again, with Mr Stewart and the ordinary boy looking on. He scarcely knew what keys he was hitting.

The screen said. IF
IF YOU
IF YOU DON'T
Maurice had broken out in a cold sweat.

"Now what's the first mistake you've made there, Maurice?"

"No line numbers, Mr Stewart."

"All right. Start again. I'll be back in a minute –"

IF YOU DON'T COME TO US. THEN WE'LL COME TO YOU.

"We need something to clear the air," said Mrs Wray to Mrs Bollom, outside the library at the end of the school day. "You wouldn't think it could get so muggy up on top of this hill."

While their mother gossiped with her friend the librarian, the ordinary boy let Ghengis chase him round the car park. Maurice, who had lost all shame, sidled up and joined in. He was hoping the rain that threatened would start, so he'd have a reasonable excuse to cadge a lift home in Mrs Bollom's car. The ordinary boy was very happy to share the fun of looking after his sister.

If only he wouldn't keep asking how Maurice made the computer do tricks like that.

They were moved on from the car park, and played tig in the derelict outdoor classroom. Ghengis was it. She didn't understand any rules – it was just like being chased by a wild animal, but at least she was using up some particles of her hyperactivity.

Ghengis roared and flung herself in wild leaps. Maurice tried to lose himself in the game. But he kept seeing that message on the computer screen, written on his brain in letters of green fire. "If you don't come to us, we'll come to you." It must be something to do with electronics. Chemical patterns forming electronic waves. Nothing to be afraid of . . . .

Ghengis chuckled. She was growling. She flexed her claws, pretending to be a tiger. She advanced on Maurice. But she wasn't looking at him. She was looking, with a tigerish scowl, at something in the hedge behind him.

"Innit getting dark," said the ordinary boy suddenly.

Maurice remembered, with an unpleasant start, the nervous cat in Aztec city. The school forecourt, where teachers were hurrying to their cars and pupils yelling and chatting as they surged towards the gates, seemed suddenly very far away. He felt horribly reluctant to turn his head.

Ghengis wasn't scared. But whatever she could see, she didn't like it. She flexed her little claws and made a fierce rush –

With a helpless moan, Maurice pitched himself forward and brought her down in full flight: in what, although he'd never been on a rugby field, was quite a creditable flying tackle.

WHAH! WHAH!

He spent the next ten minutes trying to explain himself. It wasn't easy. Even the ordinary boy had never made any serious attempt to murder his sister, trial though she was. It didn't seem the right moment to ask for a lift home. The only person who wasn't horrified with Maurice's rough tactics was Ghengis herself. She gave him a beaming smile – cutting herself off in mid howl – as she was led away.

He heard her telling her mother excitedly. "There was a real monster, Mum. I was going to EAT it!"

There was no chance, fortunately, that anyone would believe her.

He went home on the bus, thinking very uncomfortable thoughts. Much as he disliked school, he couldn't let this sort of scariness go on. It was one thing being locked in at the zoo, it was another thing when your presence became a danger to the animals. He was amazed at Ghengis's bravery. He couldn't have turned to face whatever she saw in the hedge for anyone alive.

Although of course there was some natural explanation. Electricity or something.

I'll have to switch it off, he thought. That's it. It's a kind of circuit I've set up by time-travelling. I just have to find a way to break the contact.

The promised thunderstorm had begun. Rain was crashing down now, making the streets as dark as if it was November. At least today the gloom was real, not like those shadows that gathered in Fairsea library when Maurice's historical drawings were being admired.

Maurice glanced behind him, reassured by the squashed bodies of homeward bound citizens. Had he been talking to himself out loud? He had a feeling people were looking at him. The bus was very crowded. Figures pressed together in the aisle: wet umbrellas, shopping bags, solemn faces – Maurice turned round again quickly. He didn't want to count the standing travellers. He had an uneasy feeling it would come to more than the bus company allowed. Go away, he thought silently. You're not real. But they didn't answer. They just watched, and waited.

The next day was fine and bright again. That evening he went into Aunt Ada's garden. He paced along the side of the lawn, where a darker square was outlined in the neatly cut grass. This was where an older shed must have been, before the new prefabricated one against the cemetery wall was put up.

Aunt Ada was spraying greenfly with warm soapy water.

"Was this where his laboratory was?"

"Yes, Maurice. That's right."

"What happened to it?"

"I had it taken down," she answered calmly. "I am surprised that the traces are still visible. I had to have the ground thoroughly dug out, and new topsoil laid. Nothing would grow."

"Why did you do that?" demanded Maurice. "I mean – I should have thought you'd have wanted to keep his laboratory."

She smiled placidly. "It was such a big shed. It made the garden very dark and poky."

"Wasn't there another reason? Like – when you burned the remains of his papers? You must have read something in them –"

"Oh, I didn't read anything," murmured Aunt Ada. "And if I had, Maurice, it was so long ago I'm afraid I wouldn't remember."

She nodded at him, a spidery little figure in her faded drooping cardigan. "I hope you've settled into your room," she remarked kindly, and wandered off to attend to another rosebush.

He went into the parlour. It was hot and full of sunlight. The clematis that grew up the front wall of the house tapped papery purple faces against the window. Maurice sat down at the old piano. He might as well accept it. Aunt Ada was useless to him. Whatever secret reason she had for visiting the cemetery, it had nothing to do with the things that happened to Maurice there. He'd been wrong to think she was stuck forty years ago. She'd got so old time didn't matter to her at all. She probably didn't even know what year it was. All she cared about was the aphids on the roses.

And if she did know anything, she wouldn't tell. That's probably why the Professor liked her, he thought. Probably why he left her the house. In appreciation of the way she minds her own business.

Who could he turn to now? Professor Baxter's married daughter in Oxford? Hardly. Even if she was still alive, she had just thought the old man was dotty.

There was a bowl of sweet william and gypsy grass on the round table: July flowers, ragged and bright. He picked up the portrait of young Professor Baxter, slipped the mottled envelope out of its back and looked again at those "fake" photographs. Pictures of a girl with dark hair, barefoot and wearing fancy dress. It seemed to be the same girl at the same age in all the different gardens, right from 1898 to 1939.

Maurice heaved a sigh of annoyance, reluctantly accepting the scientific evidence. All the pictures were of Moth, of course.

He didn't care to go into the Garden on his own now. He waited for Sunday when there were people about – disturbing the quietness with their cut flowers and hats and special miserable voices. He bought a bunch of yellow chrysanthemums from a barrow at the gothic gates, to disguise himself, and slipped in with a family of mourners. It comforted him to behave as if he was in a spy film. He didn't think he was spotted, or if he was there was nothing the enemy could do. It was like visiting time in hospital, when everyone has to get back into bed and lie quietly and say thank you for the grapes: leaving off all kinds of games and rows and interesting business, until the intruders have gone.

Two old ladies were sitting on the Colonel. A woman in a silly hat was down on her knees clearing all the snailshells from the thrushes' favourite smashing stone. Someone else had a trowel and was digging up the careless bright-eyed weeds to make room for a stupid begonia. The weeping ash tree with its trailing tentacle branches, which Maurice had felt sorry for in the Spring; was in full leaf now. He hid under it and looked out at the invaders through a whispering curtain. For a moment he forgot he was on a secret mission in disguise and clutched the flowers in confusion. He'd never been in this place when it was working before. Instinct had kept him away – just as he and Moth always avoided the funeral church in the valley when there were banks of flowers outside it, and the dark cars came crawling up the drive. Which is the real garden, he thought? Ours or theirs? The ash leaves touched his face – he pulled himself together and slipped out, keeping to the paths where there were most people, across to the shrubbery steps.

"Moth?" he called. "Moth?"

But there was a family coming up from the church. They stared at Maurice curiously as he stood there under the chestnut tree holding his stiff yellow flowers.

"Have you lost your way, sonny?"

"No – I'm all right."

"Sssh. Leave him alone. He looks a bit upset."

When he thought they had gone he started to call again. He could see nothing but bright, dim, unbroken greenness. He heard a twig crack and turned in relief, but it was only the little girl from the family, staring at him with her finger in her mouth.

"Here you are," said Maurice. "You have them."

He stuck the chrysanthemums in her hand and left the cemetery, walking fast with his head down. It was almost worse than being chased by shadows.

She did not come. He waited hopefully in his aunt's garden until the sky began to turn from sunset pink to a dull green. It was a good evening for insects. There were crowds of little shadowy things fluttering over the nightscented stock, and around Aunt's roses. But not the Moth he was looking for. Maurice decided he didn't like them, and went indoors. She did not appear in the house either. However, he was not entirely deserted. There were people on the landing, whispering, all through the night. He heard them stealthily fumbling with his door, and twice he switched on the light in time to see the doorknob move.

On Monday there was Junior School Sports Day. It was a major event, for which the whole first, second and third years went to the all-weather track in the town centre to watch each other run up and down and jump over things. A lot of parents came too. Fun was had by all. The third year programme went on past the end of the school day, but unfortunately the first and second year programme did not. Authority had decreed that unless handed over to parents, they had to be bussed back to school before they could go home "because of what happened last year"

Maurice's bus broke down. Its passengers had to crawl up Fairsea Hill in a crocodile, two by two, guarded by overheated and bad-tempered teachers. Jasmin Kapoor was also on Maurice's bus. A few third years had been allowed to come back, because they had no part in the remaining events. Jasmin did not play games in public, because of her religion. The big dark car would be waiting for her at Fairsea.

Needless to say, Maurice had had nothing to do with the running and jumping either. He had always refused to take seriously the idea that physical activity is actually good for asthma sufferers.

Jasmin walked beside him of her own accord. "This is utterly ridiculous. Why can't we walk on our own? Let the little beasts who want to escape, escape –"

Maurice dragged himself out of his anxious secret thoughts, and gazed at her helplessly. How strange that he should be walking along like this, practically arm in arm with Jasmin Kapoor. And it meant nothing to him at all. Too late . . . .

"Maurice?"

Something hard and spiky had just smacked Maurice on his right cheek. He retrieved the object from inside his shirt collar: it was a tiny prickly green conker.

The cemetery wall was beside them, but Jasmin clearly could not see two dirty bare feet dangling from under the overhanging leaves. An expression of alarm appeared in her eyes. She was probably afraid Maurice was about to throw another fit.

"Do you feel ill?"

"I'm fine. Just – leave me alone."

"Come on, Maurice," cried a familiar cheeky voice. "Over the wall."

She must be joking. He stared after Jasmin's back in bitter regret. Mr Groves, one of the short tempered escort guards, had already turned to scowl – Maurice hurried on: but when the crocodile went past the Garden gates he frantically ducked inside.

No one noticed. She was waiting for him on the lawn, sitting with her knees up to her chin on Felicia May Dalton, Beloved Wife and Mother, with daisies threaded in her hair. The grey squirrels jumped down and scampered away as Maurice approached, and a blackbird in a panic ran off into a holly bush.

"Silly things," said Moth. "They're always forgetting they can fly."

"Moth – I need your help."

He began to explain. He knew he had to do it quickly, before she was distracted by a passing bumblebee.

"Look, Moth. There's something buried in this cemetery —"

Moth gave him a sly sidelong glance, and giggled.

"All right, very funny. But you know what I mean. I used to think I'd found a weird place in here: some kind of space-time gateway. Now I know that Professor Baxter invented something. It allowed him to sort of listen in on people in the past. Real, genuine time-travel. But there are side effects — and the Professor was scared of them. So he got rid of his invention."

"I have buried it," murmured Moth. "What more can I do?"

He looked at her suspiciously, wondering when she had read the diary. But perhaps she had her own ways of listening in. Moth was taking daisies from her hair, and poking them between her bare toes.

"That's right. Now I don't know exactly what the invention is. It might be — headphones, or something electrical. But I know where it is. You know too. I switched it on, accidentally, when I started going to sit there. Now I want you to help me dig it up and switch it off."

Moth wriggled her toes, admiring the effect.

"Perhaps," she suggested, "if you leave them alone, they'll stop bothering you after a while."

He wished she wouldn't talk in that unscientific way. It made him remember the message on the computer screen. And the way Professor Baxter suffered from "persecution mania" even after his family took him away to Oxford. But he was still determined not to give up his time-travel.

"Professor Baxter was working in the dark ages," he said firmly. "When it comes to the chemistry of the brain and things like that. Quite likely, once modern scientists understand his discovery, it'll be easy to get rid of the unwanted side effects. People will be able to experience the past! There's nothing wrong in that . . . ."

He broke off and glanced around the lawn nervously. Trust

Moth to be stupid and childish. She was only looking at him like that to scare him. A woodpigeon crooned and crooned deep in the valley.

"*Moth*. You remember the Professor, don't you? He took pictures of you. You liked that. Don't you want to help make him famous?"

"But why do you need help? You're only going to dig a little hole."

Maurice swallowed. He didn't feel like going back to that hollow alone. Not until whatever it was was switched off. But he wasn't going to admit this to Moth.

"You're to stand guard. The gardeners might come by. If they did you would distract them. You'd enjoy that."

She slipped him another bright, sly sideways look, and nodded.

The lawn had changed while they were talking. The July sunshine seemed to have faded: although there should be hours of daylight left. Maurice remembered suddenly that Felicia May Dalton was not to be trusted. He jumped up.

"I've got to go. I have to report back at school. Be there tomorrow. About four o'clock."

The next day he was very matter of fact. He had a trowel. He found Moth sitting crosslegged at the foot of the broken Celtic cross. She had robbed a spike of foxgloves and was playing finger puppets with the flowers.

"I don't think you should do this, Maurice," she said. "I think you'll be sorry."

"I'm not interested in your opinion. Just keep watch."

"He's a silly boy, isn't he?" squeaked one of the purple fox paws.

"Yes, he's a very silly boy."

Moth's fingers wriggled, but it wasn't quite clear where the thin little voices were coming from. Maurice winced.

"Stop messing around. Go down the path a bit."

She went. Maurice could hear a lawnmower rattling quietly

but it was safely in the distance. *Alas for him who never sees the stars shine through his cypress trees* . . . He couldn't remember the rest of the poem. And whatever happened to the score table of popular inscriptions? How fearfully long ago all that seemed.

He was half afraid some sinister influence would force him to sit down and close his eyes. But if it was there, he resisted it. On his knees, he marked out a square of turf with the edge of the trowel. He hoped the invention wasn't buried too deeply. He began to prise up the grass: taking care so that he could put it back afterwards. The mower, he noticed, had stopped. By a piece of bad luck, the gardeners seemed to have found something to do by the Columbarium; he could hear their voices.

He hacked viciously at the web of springy grass roots, and heard voices coming closer. What on earth could be bringing them down this neglected path? Moth, he cried silently. Come on – do your stuff. But the voices came on instead: Mr Kidder and one of his young assistants.

"What d'you think it was?" said the young voice.

"Dunno. A pink budgie, I reckon."

"It went down here. Watch out – there's not much of a path."

"It's a tame bird. Nearly sat on my shoulder, didn't it. The wild ones'll peck it to death if we don't catch it . . . ."

Maurice was kneeling with his mouth dropped open, stunned by this bare-faced treachery. He could not see any "pink budgie" but he guessed there was one around somewhere, laughing her silly head off. He hoped she choked. In his panic he didn't have the sense to run. He ripped back the turf and began to throw up earth frantically, wielding the trowel with both hands.

"Some little child may be fretting –" said a kind but rather breathless voice. Mr Kidder broke through the tangles. Maurice gaped at him.

"Hey!" exclaimed the gardener. "Hey, you. Get out of that!"

"Bloody hell. He's desecrating the graves!"

It is not a good idea to be caught digging unauthorised holes in a cemetery. Maurice was grabbed, shaken, threatened. The only thing that saved him was that he began to wheeze. He didn't have to put it on at all, he was completely at their mercy. But Mr Kidder's nerve was shaken. Maurice got his trowel back, and was escorted, heaving noisily, to the gate. Don't ever let me catch you again . . . .

He went back alone the next day. He only needed five minutes. He was sure he had struck something that chimed, like metal or glass, just before he was interrupted. He was ready to make a quick retreat if Mr Kidder was about. On the lawn he saw a bunch of large youths gathered around Felicia May Dalton, smoking cigarettes and laughing pointlessly. Maurice gave them a wide berth. Good, he thought. They'll be my early warning system.

He peeled away the turf that Mr Kidder had angrily stamped back into place, and began to scrape carefully. Suddenly there was a crashing and smashing of green branches. A huge young man with hardly any hair appeared out of the trees.

"What's the idea?"

"What?"

"Do not attempt to deceive me," said the skinhead. (The expressions he used were less polite) "Where's your mate? The one that was fooling around (or words to that effect) up in the tree, chucking things."

"Where's his mate?" The youths stood in a grinning ring now, all around the hollow. They agreed that Maurice was not the hooligan who had disturbed them. But he would do just as well.

"All right, Tarzan. Let's see you swing from another branch."

He lost the trowel permanently that time.

Eight

Something very alarming happened to Maurice after he failed the second time to dig up Professor Baxter's time machine. It was Friday night. He was going to bed. He was sitting on the side of it (his bed) carefully applying drops of a new hydrocortisone cream to a large raw welt on his left ankle. He had several puffy, nasty looking places on his arms and legs at the moment. He must have been collecting insect bites while he was digging in King Death's Garden. He squeezed the hydrocortisone, remembering it was dangerous to exceed the stated dose . . . .

He was sitting in a carriage. He had time travelled enough by now to recognise the rocking, swaying motion; and the rumble and jangle of horses' hooves and harness. He looked down at his own hands – a man's hands in gloves of thin yellow leather. They were propped together on the polished head of a walking stick, that swayed as the carriage swayed. A few inches away from his knees he saw an expanse of skirt, dark red, with black loops and ruffles. He didn't dare raise his eyes, in case the woman saw Maurice, staring out of the face opposite her, instead of the person she expected to see. He sat there swaying, feeling paralysed, trapped in this strange body like an animal in a cage.

The carriage turned into a gravel drive, between high hedges. He helped the lady in the crinoline get down, they walked into the house . . . . It went on and on. There was no escape. He was this person, living with his sister; and with servants dressed in black and white. He sat in a room with an enormous desk, reading a newspaper, while a girl about Maurice's age crawled around making up the fire in his hearth. He walked on his lawn, and heard beside him the sound of a crinoline brushing against the grass. The person that he was probably talked, behaved normally, but Maurice wasn't aware of that. He never saw another face. Occasionally he would glimpse, out of a window or as they were driving along in the carriage, the unchanged outline of the downs against the sky. It was as if he had been kidnapped and glimpsed familiar countryside out of the window of his prison.

He woke up at last, lying in bed in his pyjamas. Nowhere near the green hollow. Once Maurice had wondered if he was eavesdropping on what was going on in someone else's dream: borrowing someone else's mind. Now it was the other way round. The doorknob did not rattle that night and no one whispered impatiently outside the door. Maurice kept the light on and tried to watch all corners of his bright shadowless room at once. He was afraid to go back to sleep.

In daylight he read bits of the diary again. It wasn't time travel itself, he noticed, that interested the Professor. It was the fact that this amazing feat could be done. That was the exciting part, the "process of transference". Until, at last, he realised the "process" had gone too far.

. . . *once more I woke with no memory. And yet I am certain the experiences continue. They feed on me as once I fed on them.*

Without a doubt, I was seriously mistaken in the strength of my second distillation. It is now many months since my last active experiments, and still the effects continue, like the phantasms produced by a powerful drug. I am thankful that Miss Drew shows no sign of sharing my ordeal, though once this disturbed me greatly and caused me to doubt my own sanity. I would not wish her to share this company. I walked through the Garden again today (I must face my fear). It was dark, cold. The birds were behaving strangely. They gather on the stones, very black, and mutter to one another. Starlings, I suppose. What do they want? . . . .

Someone was using a power drill in one of the houses down the hill. Maurice could hear children, visiting grandparents perhaps, running up and down and shouting in the quiet street. The date on the diary entry was in June 1945. The end of the war. In a couple of months, the Americans would drop a bomb on Hiroshima – but Professor Baxter would not know or care. Maurice looked up, shivering in the warm afternoon. This was a different kind of seeing into the past. The pages after June were empty. *Distillation?* He didn't remember noticing that word before. He didn't like the sound of it much. As he picked up the book to put it away a small piece of yellow newspaper fluttered out. *Ugly Disturbance in Ancient Graveyard* . . . It was a story about mysterious goings on in the graveyard of a mediaeval church in Oxford. There was no mention of any Professor Baxter, nor did it say in detail what had happened to the graves. But the date was suggestive . . . So that was where the hints of long distance time travel came from. Somebody had written across the cutting, in the same handwriting as the diary but bolder, stronger: PREJUDICE! At a later date, with different ink, the word had been crossed out.

That was Saturday. On Sunday Maurice had the brilliant idea of writing to his parents and telling them all about it. Mum was a pretty sensible person, she was very good at dealing with problems sometimes. Luckily, on Sunday night he realised that this brilliant idea was a disaster and could only result in Maurice being moved from Fairsea to a rather different establishment. *And perhaps the shadows would follow him there, the shadows would be with him in there.* He tore the letter up in horror.

By Monday he had plucked up the courage to have another

go at treasure hunting. He'd decided that the best thing to do with whatever he found was to pack it up carefully and send it to Caltec. They had never answered the letter he sent describing his time-travel experience, but they still seemed like the best people to deal with something on the frontiers of human knowledge. Not only because they were Americans, and more likely to be open minded than stuffy English scientists but also, to be honest, because California was a good long way away. How should I pack it? he wondered. He would have to protect himself, and the Post Office, from unwanted plunges into the Victorian era. A lead-lined box would be best. Lead held in even radioactivity. He trembled at the thought of the cost of posting a lead box to America . . . .

He looked up and found he had been so busy thinking he had missed his way. He must have taken the wrong turn after the Columbarium, he was back on the lawn again. He retraced his steps. Here were the rosebeds, grown into a thick leafy maze now, the foliage such a dark and shiny green it looked black in the sun. The roses were all in order, white and orange and red. And here, of course, was the path that led away, with gravel growing mossy and the grass creeping in on either side. There were a lot of blackbirds – or something – scratching around in the undergrowth. Maurice took no notice. He walked on firmly, clutching his briefcase. And here was the hollow. Stupid, of course you couldn't possibly get lost.

But he had.

It was a hollow, but not the right one. He had never seen this place before. There was an enormous white tomb in the middle of this green depression. It proved, on inspection, to be the memorial of a railway engineer. Maurice walked round it several times. In the first startled moment he thought it was a hallucination. But it was real. There was a heap of lawn mowings beside it; clearly the gardeners were no strangers here. Still he found himself looking for a hole in the turf, or a place that looked disturbed. There was none. And all the while "blackbirds" scuffled suggestively and branches rubbed against each other in the breeze, sounding like whispering voices. There was no breeze.

He went back to the lawn and tried again. But he just couldn't seem to get on the right track. Paths began and ended nowhere at this end of the cemetery, and the graves were a jumble. It could be that he was more frightened than he cared to admit, and he was just confusing himself. But it was well past five by the funeral church clock and as the Professor said a summer day could seem dark and cold. He decided not to push his luck.

The term was ending at Fairsea as at every other school. The ordinary boy had forgiven Maurice for rugby tackling Ghengis. He confessed that the thought of the long summer holidays in her company was almost more than he could bear. She bit him when he wouldn't pretend to be a monster, and being hyperactive she had the strength of ten. Maurice's flight was booked to join his family in the Gulf, and when he got there they were all going to go away on holiday to an Arabian seaside resort. In September he would start his career at the International School. Auntie Sue and Uncle Tom fussed over the arrangements. Just a few months ago, the very mention of the International School had been almost enough to put Maurice in hospital. But now all this, the ordinary boy, Ghengis, the end of term, passed him by. It was like a dream, none of it seemed to matter.

He was quite sure he had invisible company all the time now. He heard whispering behind his back at school and in broad daylight. He was terrified he was going to find himself answering out loud. They waited for him in the folds of the curtains at Aunt's parlour door, they waited on the dark stairs. They were in his room at night. And each morning he woke up feeling mysteriously tired, from strange vivid dreams which he forgot the moment he opened his eyes.

He managed to persuade Jasmin to come into the cemetery with him, instead of going to the library after school. He felt he could trust her, at least partly.

"It's just a place I can't find," he explained awkwardly. "I want to see if you can't find it either."

She wasn't very cooperative but she let herself be led across the lawn and up and down in between the ivied trees. They found the white mausoleum of the railway engineer, they even got down to the fringes of the Aztec city. But the magic carpet remained obstinately hidden. At five o'clock Jasmin refused to stay any longer. She stood on the path between two red rosebeds, and rubbed her hands up and down her thin arms.

"It's creepy in here," she said. "I don't want to upset you, Maurice, but it is creepy. My arms have gone goosepimpled. I feel cold."

"It isn't always like this," he told her. "It's peaceful really. You'd like it. I mean, you would have liked it –"

Jasmin stared at him with more sympathy than irritation. "You're a funny boy, Maurice," she said. "I don't know what to make of you. I've given up seeing Aziz, you know. I've always meant to say – thank you for not spreading it round the school."

It would have been a dream come true once, to be alone with Jasmin Kapoor like this. Just as he'd planned. They would be friends, kindred spirits; nothing coarse about it. Although later their friendship might develop . . . . But it was not real any more. He had given up all that world, to be a time-traveller.

"Did you fall out with him?" he asked lamely.

"No." She shrugged her shoulders, looking gloomily at the rosebushes. "It just wasn't worth it."

Maurice couldn't think of anything to say. He had a glimpse of what life might be like for Jasmin Kapoor. Being called a wog and "that coloured girl". And at the end of every day of that treatment the big dark car swallowed her up, like another sort of prison. At least Maurice had been promised he would grow out of some of his problems. He wanted to tell her – I hope you escape. But Jasmin was at the wrong end of a telescope. He had other things on his mind.

"I've got to go now, the car will be waiting. They don't like me to be late."

She turned back as she walked away. "I'm sorry you're leaving. But I bet the International School's better than Fairsea."

Leaving? thought Maurice, puzzled. Am I? I suppose I am. But he couldn't imagine it. The plane flight, packing, the Do'an . . . he couldn't concentrate on any of that.

Jasmin was right, the afternoon had turned chilly. He walked down the Columbarium steps and up the main drive, past the horse statue and the family who lived under a skating rink. Nothing crept behind him or darted out of sight when he turned his head, but he didn't feel any relief. There was a heaviness in the air like the threatening quiet just before a thunderstorm. In the upper graveyard the gardeners had been at work. The tall flowering grass had got out of hand, overwhelming everything. It had to be dealt with. Maurice walked through bleached dead poisoned stubble, with gravestones standing up in it like strange shaped rocks silhouetted against a gloomy sky. Birds were gathering. They must be upset by the sudden lack of cover, and the loss of all the insects in the grass. They sat in rows on the tops of the stones, crowding each other and flapping their wings. There were a lot of them, more than Maurice had ever seen in here before. Starlings, he thought. Is that what they are? He remembered the diary, and shivered.

Mary was worried. She sat over him while he had his tea and tried to make him eat. He was rude to her and angry but she didn't take any notice. He escaped to his room but she followed him there.

"Where's my washing up gloves, Maurice? You seen them? You been using them for anything?"

She barged into the room, and exclaimed loudly. Maurice's window, which was always kept shut, had been opened wide.

"What the idea, Maurice? Didn't you see that pollen

forecast in the paper this morning? Are you aiming deliberately to get yourself sick?"

"Pollen doesn't give me asthma." But he couldn't work up any enthusiasm for the argument.

She pulled the window down firmly.

"Don't you touch that again. Now what about my gloves?"

"I don't know anything about the washing up gloves. Who paid for them anyway? You or Aunt Ada? You're not supposed to take them home with you."

When he turned round from glaring her out of the door, Moth was sitting on his chest of drawers.

"Moth! How did you get in here?"

"I flew in through the window, stupid. Isn't that why you left it open?"

She fiddled with the coloured pins on his map, not yet dismantled, of the Middle East. She was smirking triumphantly. It was hard to bear.

"All right. I know you can help me if you want to. Or have you just come to say I told you so, you little brute."

"I did say you shouldn't pick the flowers."

She giggled. "Maurice, have you still got that camera you told me about?"

"What's that got to do with anything?"

"Oh, well, if you don't want to be nice –" sighed Moth, with her eye on the window.

Maurice groaned. "All right, all right. I'll take your picture, I promise."

She gave him a beaming smile, full of wicked little pointy teeth. "It's quite simple. All you have to do is go in there at night time. Things are different then, in the Garden."

"You mean I'll be able to find the place, and dig up whatever's there?"

"Things are different, after dark," said Moth. "Do you want to come now? We could climb over the wall."

But this was too much to face. After a few false starts he managed to say "Er – no, not right now. I've got a better idea.

I'll meet you there tomorrow, after school. We can just stay in after the gates are shut."

She was waiting on the lawn, as before.

"We're all right," he said briskly. "I told Aunt Ada I was going to have tea at a friend's house."

He had never bothered to explain himself to his great aunt before. But if the operation had to be done in darkness he wouldn't be home for hours, and she might think that odd, since he didn't usually go anywhere in the evenings.

Moth was teasing a ladybird on Felicia May Dalton's back.

"What did she say?"

"She said – be sure and take your survival kit, Maurice."

He smiled wryly. His survival kit had changed a bit. He had his inhaler, and a picnic of gluten free bread; a torch, a large tablespoon, a pair of washing up gloves and an extra heavy duty dustbin bag, folded up small.

"What do we do now? Sit and wait?"

Moth skipped to her feet. "Follow me, Maurice. I'll show you things."

The afternoon was warm and bright, without shadows. King Death's Garden was as it had been before, when he and Moth first used to explore it together. They found the black and white tom cat and chased him without mercy, they watched a fat red and yellow spider stringing her new web across a bramble bush. Moth parted the long grass down in Aztec city, and uncovered little trodden thoroughfares crossing and joining each other – the mouse underground. She found the holes where the mice were hiding from daylight, and wickedly stopped them up with flowerheads pulled off the elder bushes. She had a prize she had been saving: a magpie's nest that had fallen out of one of the big elm trees. It looked like nothing but a spiky bundle of twigs, but when she pulled it open it was hollow inside. She dipped in her hand and brought out a scrap of purple ribbon from a wreath, three bits of silver paper from cigarette packets, a keyring, a small length of copper wire and a blackened coin that turned out to be an old sixpence.

"Magpies like collecting things" said Moth. "Just like you, Maurice" – and she laughed and raced away.

Maurice looked at the odd collection of rubbish and felt annoyed. But Moth had vanished. He hurried after, afraid she'd gone off to torment the gardeners. She seemed to have completely forgotten this was a serious occasion.

But the gardeners were all back at the office putting their tools away. Moth came to rest on the slope under the upper graveyard wall, sitting on the kerb of a grave that was planted with red and orange snapdragons. Maurice sat nearby, chewing a grass-stalk.

Bzzz.

She had trapped a bumblebee inside one of the flowers. Suddenly Maurice started. He looked up, he looked around. What had changed? The sky was still blue, but it looked deeper, and the grass was greener, and the innocent shadows meant something more. A woodpigeon was shouting away, down in the valley.

"Now the gate is shut" said Moth softly.

He felt frightened then, remembering the last time he was locked in here, when Moth herself had been worried and in a hurry to get him over the wall. But the fear didn't last. I'll find out what happens, he thought, with a shiver down his back. They could walk the paths now, without being afraid of meeting the gardeners. Moth danced and flitted and played irreverent hopscotch. Maurice wandered after her in the gathering twilight, feeling strangely at home. He met the tom cat, which stopped and looked at him with different, deeper eyes. Everything seemed to be coming awake, even the trees and flowers were more alive, more conscious. They all looked as if they were nodding and winking, maybe jumping up and changing places behind his back. But he didn't mind. It was exciting. Just a little longer in this mysterious world, and he would be able to flit about like Moth, dance on the graves, *be* one of the things with peering eyes, hopping and hiding . . . .

An owl hooted, and another answered. Moth and Maurice were back where they had been when the gates were locked, sitting quietly on the slope overlooking the dim valley. In the west, a few tiny streaks of red were fading in a deep sea-coloured sky. Something black and small whipped across the sea-colour, dipped at the edge of the trees and came flickering back over their heads. Maurice ducked, unnecessarily.

"Bats," whispered Moth. "Would you like to ride on a bat's back?"

The owls hooted again, and the last threads of sunset vanished.

"Now it is night," said Moth.

Maurice sat up straight. He grasped his plastic carrier bag, that he had been trailing round with him all this time. It's quite simple, he thought. But I'll be glad when it's over. The smooth turf they were sitting on was dotted with graves and evergreen bushes. He could still see quite clearly . . . . Suddenly he drew a sharp breath. He had glimpsed a crouching shape, just slipping behind a clump of cypresses. The tom cat? No, it wasn't the tom cat. There was another, sneaking out of sight. The hairs on the back of Maurice's neck jumped up like porcupine quills. He looked at Moth accusingly.

She laughed.

"What are they doing here, Moth? You said it would be safe –"

"No, I didn't."

There was an awful silence. Maurice noticed with a shock how far he'd let himself slip into unscientific thinking. Of course Moth couldn't promise anything about those shadows. They didn't exist, except in Maurice's head. They were just strange side effects . . . . But in that case why was he here? He stood up sharply – but then he had to sit down. His knees had turned to unscientific jelly.

"There's nothing there," he quavered, in what was supposed to be a loud confident voice. "Just – chemical patterns.

Images from the past, somehow regenerated . . . ."

"Oh yes, I know," agreed Moth cheerfully. "My Professor took them out of the Garden and regenerated them in his shed. But if you want to go on playing with them, Maurice, there's no need to dig anything up. That's silly. All you have to do is just stay in here. That's what they want. And you want it too, don't you? You don't want to go to the Do'an."

Maurice stood up again. But it was no good. How could a wheezing asthmatic wimp hope to get away?

And did he really want to? Perhaps Moth was right . . . .

Travelling in time was so much better than being at Fairsea. So much better than the miserable fate of being dragged away to the Middle East. He'd rather be almost anyone, dead or alive, than Maurice Eastman, and that was the truth. When he was time-travelling he didn't have asthma or plagues of boils. Nobody sneered at him. It would have been good to be rich and famous, to pay people out. But he didn't really mind about that. If everybody knew about the time–travel, it wouldn't belong to Maurice anymore. He tried to think of one solitary thing in what people called the real world, that was worth screaming and running for. Because that was what he'd have to do. Scream and run. And he couldn't run. He didn't have the strength.

He had come through the mysterious world of twilight, neither one thing nor the other. Now the real night was waiting. Exciting, fascinating. A scientist shouldn't be afraid to make any experiment. After all, the shadowy things hadn't done anything to him, except invade his mind. They had a right to claim him, it would be stupid to run away. He had woken them up and now he could be their eyes. Fresh eyes, a fresh mind to touch and feel the worlds of the past . . . .

Moth was still sitting beside him, her eyes bright in the clear summer darkness. Her dress, which was the deep red of a July rose, looked purple now where you could see any colour at all. She was watching him with the same heartless, interested, look that he remembered from when they watched the tom cat kill the fieldmouse.

"I won't be able to play about like that any more," thought Maurice regretfully. "Not in the daytime anyway, I suppose. I'll be d—"

He felt as if he had pulled himself up on the edge of a fearful cliff.

His heart began to beat very fast. He was afraid he wasn't going to be able to breathe. And the things that were d— and wanted him to be d— too, were watching, waiting. Not "harmless chemical patterns" after all. Oh, he had known it from the first, only he just didn't like the word.

Dead.

"Moth – how could you! You knew this was going to happen!"

Moth pouted. "You're just like my Professor," she said sulkily. "You don't want to play with me. You just want to collect rubbish."

She giggled. "Now the rubbish is going to collect you, and it serves you right."

Maurice didn't believe in ghosts. Right from the start when he was wandering round King Death's Garden collecting inscriptions he had been pleased with himself because he was too intelligent to find a place of this kind frightening. And when he realised – partially – what was happening to him when he was carried away by the magic carpet of Death's flowers, he had managed not to give way to stupid prejudices. All right, the people whose lives he dreamed were not alive anymore. Nor was anybody in the past alive in the present. It never worried Doctor Who.

He had managed not to think about the actual graves, about the actual contents of the graves, in connection with Professor Baxter's time machine. Now he remembered a list of names and dates. Stupid ignorant people like Mary would say it was very nasty stuff. He was prepared, suddenly, to admit they might have a point. Nobody likes to be spied on. People who've been left to rest in peace probably have a right to expect just that . . . .

He licked his dry lips. "Look –" he croaked, not to Moth but to the accusing shadows. "I'm really sorry. I know it was wrong. I won't dig you up and send you to Caltec. I won't bother you ever again. Just let me go –"

His words faded away strangely, but the unwanted, unseen company remained. Moth laughed.

"You can't talk to them, Maurice. They aren't people, they're just leftovers. I don't know what happens to the real people planted in the Garden, I never see them."

It was not pitch dark. It was a clear night, with the afterglow of sunset still in the sky. Maurice could see quite well. As Moth was gleefully explaining his position the word distillation came into his mind, with unpleasant force, together with the image of a boiling pot, filled with a steaming, bubbling stew – of stolen odds and ends. Everything he had refused to think, about what Professor Baxter had been up to. Hobbling maimed things with faces like leather. Things that shouldn't even be able to crawl, crawling out from behind the bushes.

"Moth –" he wailed. "What shall I do?"

No answer. The kerb of the grave was empty. She never managed to stay in one place for long. He knew he couldn't blame her for the trick she'd played on him. To Moth, everything was a joke. Even hungry ghosts.

"I'm going home," said Maurice.

It was a long walk to the upper graveyeard, forcing his reluctant legs one after the other. The shrubbery steps were dreadful. He had plenty of time to think. About the stupidity of despising the ordinary boy, of despising his own mother because she preferred playing tennis to reading a book. He'd never looked at it like that before. It was always other people who despised Maurice. The meanness and cruelty of other people; whereas Maurice of course was never mean, he was a suffering victim. Why should he expect special treatment just because he sometimes had a bit of a wheeze or a rash? His family hadn't abandoned him. He had abandoned them. Could Mum and Dad help it if there weren't any jobs in England? When you can't blame anyone in particular it's easiest just to blame everybody, and kick them all out and go and sit in a hole full of private secret things that are much more fun. Then one day – or one night – you wake up and find you are living in a can of worms.

He thought of Professor Baxter, angry and resentful because life wouldn't give him what he wanted. He must have known that what he was doing was horrible. But he wouldn't give it up, oh no. He let everything worth having just drop away from him, rather than give up his treasure. But at last he found himself alone in the dark, clutching a handful of rubbish.

He remembered his torch and switched it on, but he soon switched it off again. Better not to know. Better not to see what it was that brushed against him, or pattered behind him, or passed with a whispering breath just by his ear.

Thinking serious thoughts, and making (fervent) resolutions to be a better Maurice if he could only get out of this, made him feel quite brave. But the ordeal wasn't over yet. There was a shape darker than the night sky, crouching in the crown of the weeping ash tree. He put on the torch to make sure, and his heart began to thump very hard. The torch beam was weedy, but he could still see enough to make out a few things. The population of life sized stone angels on the way down to the office and the front gate, had increased significantly.

"No!" said Maurice, more firmly than he would have thought possible.

He turned, and began to run. He ran past the weeping ash, he ran between the ranks of shabby stubbled graves; brambles or worse than brambles tugging at his clothes. He was down the shrubbery steps and leapt five at the bottom, where something was crouching (maybe a bush). He ran round the funeral church and up the main drive, his feet bang, banging in the still echoing night. He ran through the beech trees at the bottom of the lawn and heard a bird singing as if nothing had ever gone wrong with the world since it began; and saw a pale face at his elbow, but it was behind him before he could scream. His breath was coming in bucketsful, pouring painfully into his lungs and hurling itself out again, and his knees wanted to bend the wrong way but he ran. He ran up the lawn, his feet slithering and sliding on the dewy grass – he remembered that Felicia May Dalton was not to be trusted so he veered away from the tall gates and ran again, diagonally, with his arms flailing, and stood under the wall on the Fairsea side.

He couldn't do it. He had never climbed a tree in his life and this was harder than a tree. He wouldn't even have been able to climb the little low wall over the allotments without a bench, and Moth to egg him on.

He wondered if he could stay here, with his back to the wall. So long as he didn't go to sleep – and he felt as if it would be easy to stay awake . . . . But the prospect was too terrifying. He had to get to some refuge *now*, or they would have him. He couldn't think of anywhere except – forlorn hope – the address of Mary's bedsit. He gritted his teeth and drew his breath in gasps, and he climbed. His legs and arms were shaking violently when he got to the top. He dragged himself over the coping stones. Scraping skin off his ribs because his arms hadn't the strength to lift him, he turned himself laboriously and dropped.

He had seen people do that, but knowing nothing practical he had forgotten to lower himself the length of his arms, or to look and see how high up he was. It was a long way, he realised, falling. The pavement smashed into him and he lay on it like a squashed beetle. I can't breathe! I can't breathe! He was only winded. He saw something moving at the big gateway up the hill. Maybe it was only a pair of policemen, or an innocent passerby.

He staggered to his feet and ran and ran, blundering and stumbling and never looking behind him until finally he staggered up some dirty steps of a big house in the run down streets beyond Fairsea, and fastened himself, with his last gasp, on a doorbell.

When he was able to notice his surroundings again, he was in a large untidy room, sitting on the edge of a hard bed with a blanket wrapped round his shoulders. He knew he had rung the wrong bell and caused a great fuss. Doors had banged, someone had shrieked, he had been propped up at the bottom of some stairs with his nose between his knees above a gritty rug that smelled of cats. He had heard a telephone being dialled, and he remembered gasping out wildly.

"No! Not the hospital! They'll get me. They'll get me on the way –!"

A rich and welcome voice said "Don't get scared, Maurice. I only phoning your auntie."

And now he was safe, with the tight band around his chest dissolving. The shadows were shut out. Mary had switched on her gasfire. She was behind a screen at the other end of the room, he could hear her pouring something into a mug.

"You realise I disgrace in front of these people?" she called from behind the screen. "A young man in my room at this time."

Maurice hugged the blanket and felt waves and waves of relief sweeping over him. The rough, fusty feel against his chin was real, and so was Mary's sarcastic grumbling. He was alive, things were happening to him. It didn't matter how ordinary, how stupid . . . .

Mary appeared, resplendent in a vivid red and green dressing gown.

"Get that down you."

"I hate meat extract," he complained, sniffing it.

"No argument. Boy, your hands are like ice. Where you been to get so cold?"

"I've been in the graveyard," said Maurice. It didn't occur to him to lie. He wasn't in the mood.

Mary's eye fell on the plastic carrier, which he had clutched in his mad desperation all the way. It had fallen over, and one of a pair of rubber gloves had come out, with a greasy paperbag and the end of a tablespoon. She looked from Maurice to the bag and back again.

"Hmmph," she said at last. "You been scaring yourself silly, huh? I knew you up to something, weeks ago. You been trying to raise the spirits like that old Professor, haven't you?"

Maurice blinked in the steam of his hot drink. He had a feeling the normal Maurice would be affronted at this tasteless naming of names, but he really couldn't be bothered. He remembered all the times she'd tried to warn him. He might have attempted to explain how one thing had led to another: that secretive house, the story of the mysterious scientist, the "time travel" that was so exciting. He remembered in time that whatever Mary thought about him "scaring himself", she certainly didn't know the half of it. And it was better that way . . . .

"Mary," he said at last. "What really happened? You know, with my great aunt and the Professor. Why did he leave her that house and why did she burn all his papers. And why did everybody keep telling me not to ask questions?"

Mary sighed. She looked away from him, at the bright bars of the gasfire.

"It was like this, Maurice. Your great auntie got pregnant when she was a young girl. She wasn't married. Whoever was the baby's father, he didn't stand by her and she wouldn't tell his name. She was too proud. Now you prob'ly think that's nothing terrible and in modern days you should be right. But in those days long ago her family – your mama's family, Maurice – threw her out. At which point, she comes to work for the Professor. He advertise for a respectable old single lady. She go along. She has a nerve, your great auntie. Well, he took her on. Perhaps she knows and he knows people are whispering behind their hands about the Professor too. That he is crazy or else worse.

"Well, the little girl died, Maurice. Your great auntie's family said it was a blessing. Imagine that – what a thing to say. But the Professor, he paid for the headstone. As for leaving her the house, why shouldn't he? As for burning the papers, he already burned most of them. And she didn't want him to be remembered for that nasty, crazy stuff."

She gave Maurice a stern look. He was afraid he blushed.

"You just frighten yourself for nothing, Maurice. There was no big secret. Just respect for the dead. But you don't understand about being a friend, and having respect for someone. I think you don't, Maurice. You make it very hard for anyone to be a friend to you. You going to have to change that."

The hot drink was making Maurice sleepy. He sat listening to his own wheezing breath: it was in a way a comforting familiar sound. His eyes drifted around Mary's big room, and fixed on the contents of a large wooden table. He saw knives, a bowl, a vague shaped lump of something wrapped up in damp hessian. And now he saw that the room was full of people – small figures, none of them more than half a metre high. Bending, stretching, carrying things. Some of them were modelled in clay, some carved in wood. They were beautiful. Maurice felt his face going red as a beetroot. He remembered exactly how he had smiled, when the home help had claimed to be an artist.

Mary shrugged her shoulders, and looked down at her puffy kitchen hands, planted on her heavy knees.

Far away the front door slammed and a rowdy couple stamped up the stairs, yelling at each other at the tops of their voices. Mary scowled and jumped up. She hurried to her door and could be heard muttering across the hall, to an ally. The continuing saga . . . . Maurice sipped his drink and thought of the sad story. He was ashamed of having asked Aunt Ada all those prying questions. Poor great aunt, he thought. And I thought *my* parents were rotten. Poor Maurice, he couldn't help adding. I'm always put in the wrong. I always mess up. I'm doomed –

Mary came back. She sat down again, and watched him for a moment. Then she suddenly put out her dark hand, and patted it against his cheek, smiling sadly.

"Ah, Maurice. Life so unfair, isn't it. Right down unfair."

Nine

As far as Maurice was aware his great aunt never knew that anything unusual had happened the night he stayed at Mary's. He was afraid there would be a fuss because Mary had had to ring up in the middle of the night. But it wasn't the middle of the night. It was only about ten thirty. He worked out later that his whole ghastly ordeal had probably lasted half an hour. The story was that Maurice had been overcome by asthma on the way home from wherever he'd been spending the evening. Great aunt remarked it was very sensible of him to have remembered Mary's address, and left it at that. She believed that she had done her young visitor a service, in politely ignoring his health problems as far as she possibly could. And perhaps she was right.

"Send us a postcard," said the ordinary boy.

"Okay," said Maurice.

"Bet you don't."

"Bet I do."

"Make it one of a belly dancer. Put it in an envelope, so me Mum doesn't laugh at me."

Maurice raised his eyebrows. "A belly dancer!" he sneered.

"D'you want anything written on the back, or would that be a waste of effort?"

The ordinary boy laughed noisily and thumped Maurice on the arm.

It was strange to think that he would probably never see Ghengis again. She'd have forgotten how to growl by the time Dad's home leave came up: she'd have turned into a human being. He remarked on this curious trick of time to her brother. The ordinary boy said he doubted it.

On the last day before his flight Maurice's uncle and aunt took him and the cousins to the beach for a picnic. There was supposed to have been a more exciting day out, but it got lost in the arrangements. So here they were, not a million miles from the Palace Pier, sitting on the shingle with ten thousand other people. Maurice had to keep telling his kind relatives he really didn't mind. They offered him food that had clearly been chosen with fearful care, to be luxurious and yet safely within his diet sheet. Seeing their nervous faces, and the gloomy resigned looks passing between his cousins, made Maurice feel extremely embarrassed. He understood that his company was expected to ruin any social event. It was like looking through a window at a rather nasty looking character and suddenly realising the window was a mirror.

Finding him friendlier than before, the two boy cousins (out of their parents' earshot) started telling him about Great Aunt Ada Drew's, and how they used to call it "the witchy house" when they were little. They had heard, or they'd made up, lots of stories about the old mad professor. They had been forbidden, they explained, to tell Maurice any of them when he was going to stay there, because it might have started up his asthma. What sort of stories? asked Maurice. Oh, just about the way the neighbours used to see him in the middle of the night. Coming over the wall with a sack on his shoulder. *From the other garden next door* . . . .

Maurice tried hard to look bored and sophisticated, as he said he didn't want to hear any more.

The cousins went swimming. Maurice strolled off with his jacket over his arm for a last walk down the pier. It was a warm day, though not quite as warm as all the half naked bodies would make you think. England – land of the windbreak and the tarry towel. The sea roared and slushed as always, bottle green and bubbling around the rusted iron girders.

Maurice had been back to King Death's Garden with his tablespoon. And for whatever reason, he had had no difficulty in finding the place he was looking for this time. Nobody interrupted him. If there were any unexplained shadows on the grass he didn't count them so he didn't know.

He didn't know if it made any sense or not, but he had already brought in a big bunch of gladioli and put them on the grave of someone called Pte Peter Matchell 1898–1916 of the XII rifle regiment. Died of wounds. He meant "I'm sorry." He couldn't remember any of the other names from the list in the diary, and it was gone now. He'd put it in the dustbin himself, along with the three books of Latin poetry.

There were some things that he still didn't understand. For instance – how much Aunt Ada really knew. And what about the old gentleman in tweeds? There wasn't much question about who he was – but Maurice couldn't help worrying a little about that person's present status. (Supposing there was, after all, more to him than a chemical pattern.) He just hoped that it would be all right now, and his fellow scientist would be able to settle down in his own garden, wherever that was. At rest.

"Moth," he called, to the empty air. "I'm going to get rid of this. I bet that's what you wanted me to do all along. You're right. Some flowers just aren't worth picking."

The bees buzzed in the pink valerian, a blackbird cried chack! as it flew by. There was no other answer.

The waves roared softly. The pier arcade said Ching Taka Taka Pow Zap Zap: the seagulls screeched and children yelled. Maurice thought about Mary and her kindness. He could have had a sculptress for a friend, all this time. He could have had Alec Verne for a friend, and learned about old Brighton in an honest, daylight way. Not to mention Jasmin.

Too late now. That's the price you pay, Maurice, he told himself. For going round with a bucket over your head.

He took out of his pocket a freezer bag carefully secured, containing a small antique medicine bottle. It was sealed with a mouldering plug of cork and sealing wax, and half full of brownish glistening liquid. With a regretful sigh for his brilliant scientific career, he pitched it with all the force he could muster so it smashed against a girder; and disappeared. He was sorry about the broken glass, but he felt it would have been extremely unwise to open the bottle and pour. Even in broad daylight on the Palace Pier. He looked down sadly at his own flabby white arms on the rail, still scarred with red from his last rash.

"Well," he said out loud. "That's that. From now on I'm an ordinary boy myself."

In King Death's Garden, old Miss Ada Drew got down carefully on her knees to tidy a few weeds out of the sweet alyssum. It grew in a scented mass of tiny white faces, over one small grave. She stayed there for a while, thinking resignedly that the season would soon change. The arthritis would come back in force and pin her to the house again. It was a pity, but it couldn't be helped.

"She has awakened from the dream of life," said the message on the stone.

The old lady got up, slowly. Down in the valley woodpigeons were crooning, and the trees almost drooping under their heavy freight of leaves. "Ah, summer, summer," she murmured. "And after summer, autumn. And then winter, but then spring . . . ." In a sycamore tree by the shrubbery steps Moth was rocking herself to sleep through drowsy August, dreaming of conker fights and autumn leaves.

In the apartment in Ishar, on the balcony overlooking their

swimming pool, Maurice's father opened a letter and turned the photograph that fell out this way and that.

"Look at this, Angie. He must have posted it last week. It says on the back "here is a friend of mine". Can you see the friend?"

The photograph was of Great Aunt Ada's garden, looking very summery and English with roses and sweet peas and delphiniums.

"It's good," said Maurice's mother. "Very sharp. Except for that blurry bit by the red rose bush. I think, well, I think he must mean the garden. It's poetic. Oh dear, your son's a bit deep, isn't he. I'm afraid he thinks I'm pretty stupid. I hope I can live up to him –"

But Maurice, meanwhile, was between flights in the Transit Lounge at Abu Dhabi, drinking cola (which was strictly forbidden to him) and searching in vain for a postcard of a bellydancer.